Contents

Introduction

There is no magic key which opens the box marked WRITING. Children can only learn to write by writing. It is often hard work, but hard work which brings immense rewards. It enables the child to create experiences and to explore ideas. Like reading, it opens up new worlds and is a way of reinforcing and consolidating information. As soon as the child realises that he can make meaning from marks on paper, he has become a writer.

On my visits to schools I often ask the children how many of them have done some writing that day – all hands go up – and I can truthfully say that everyone in the room is a writer. Such acknowledgement of writing as a worthwhile activity is important. This is not to suggest, however, that the skills of writing are learned by osmosis. The teacher's task is of vital importance. She must guide, advise, encourage, evaluate – and she must *teach*. Above all, as the first reader, she is in the ideal position to offer praise and congratulations to the writer. My grandmother was the appreciative audience for my own first poems. I remember her quiet praise with gratitude.

First success

The sun newly-minted
in the summer sky, the
mesmeric sound of roller
on clay, gentle pthud
thud of racquet on ball,
grandmother mouthing my
words
under her breath.

My words! I watched
her eyes, magnified to
medallions, move slowly
across the page. 'Lovely
poem,' she said, smiling.
We sat in the sun, well-pleased
one with the other.

Moira Andrew

Doreen Gabriel (National Writing Project, U.K.) says, 'We must *grow* writers in our classroom and accept their attempts as growing things to be nurtured, rather than objects to be repaired and fixed.' This philosophy underlies all the ideas and suggestions in *Words with Wings*.

1991

Aims of the writing curriculum

To encourage children to write:

  i)   on a variety of topics
  ii) with different audiences in mind, using language and style
      appropriate to each context
  iii) with a growing mastery of the framework of literacy
  iv) with some understanding of the skills of drafting and editing
  v) with enjoyment and success

Beginning Writing

Examples of copying patterns, overwriting and underwriting

Most children come to school wanting to write. They have some knowledge of the writing process and its function. A pre-school child will have watched his parents write a letter, leave a note for the milkman, sign a cheque, note down a telephone message. He wants to take part in this adult activity and add his scribble to his parents' writing. For him, at the pre-school stage, this scribble *is* writing.

When she comes to school, the young child knows that marks make writing and that, in some magic way, they communicate meaning. She can probably recognise her own name and may have had a go at copying it. Almost certainly she will understand that writing is important.

The infant teacher has the task of harnessing the child's interest in the writing process and helping him to transfer from an unco-ordinated scribble to a legible script. She has the problem of matching the manual difficulty of forming letters to the triumph of making meaning – uphill work, perhaps, but one of the most rewarding tasks in the primary school.

Writing and reading are inextricably linked. All the good practice of handling books, using picture

Beginning writing

and context clues and active listening are equally important to the beginning of writing as to the beginning of reading.

Let children make their own books from the earliest days at school. A four-paged book about the weather is an excellent starter. Write the word 'sun' at the top of the page. Ask the child to overwrite or copy the letters in wax crayons. Let him draw a picture beneath the writing. Do the same for rain, cloud, wind, snow, etc. The important idea is for the child to write a whole word which has meaning. Let him 'read' his work back. Concentrate on four-paged books, easily finished, on a number of topics, 'My friends', 'My family', 'My clothes' etc.

Alongside book-making with whole words, practise writing rhythms. To the sung or chanted rhythm of 'Humpty-Dumpty' get the children to make writing patterns. Use wax crayons or paint. These patterns can look very decorative and give the children practice in handling a writing tool (see photograph on previous page).

It is important for children to attempt blocks of letters which make up real words before they try to separate them into the intensive practice of single letters. Go for meaning-making first. When they have built up some confidence in their own ability to handle a writing tool and make marks which can be read back, only then is it time to perfect the letter forms.

I find it best to teach letters with the connector-flicks from the very beginning. This means that the children do not have to change their style of handwriting later – as they become faster and more confident the letters link to one another and become 'joined-up writing' without any trouble. I also prefer to use blank paper as I feel that young children have enough to cope with without trying to make their letters stand on the line. This is a personal preference, one with which many teachers will disagree.

Writing is about getting one's thoughts down on paper and it takes some time before many children can match dexterity of hand with speed of thought. The teacher becomes, in effect, the children's secretary at this stage. Introduce 'I can', 'I wish', 'I like' etc books (see photograph). Encourage the children to copy out the known phrase 'I like' and draw underneath. The teacher then writes in the word 'sausages' or whatever and the child either over or under-writes and reads it back. Students and interested parents can provide a great deal of assistance during this time-consuming period.

Examples of simple books in the early days at school (see previous page and page 49)

Act as secretary for story-writing and the writing of poems (see Books and Beginnings of poetry). Use a clipboard and write down the children's suggestions in a list. On a second sheet of paper begin to put the ideas into some coherent order. Read the words back. When the children are satisfied with the result, copy it out in best for a wall display or wall-story. Encourage the children to 'read' it back so that they develop the idea of marks having meaning.

In the following extract I worked with a group of four-year-olds using the above process. We looked at a travel clock and listened to it ticking. We turned it upside down, passed it from hand to hand, thought about what it sounded like, how it was used.

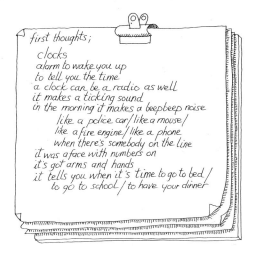

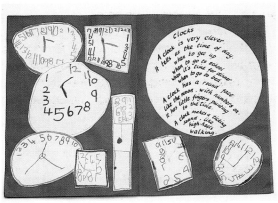

Three stages in producing finished work for display in a class book

Beginning writing

The idea of ticking sounding like 'high heels walking' was a moment of inspiration for one little boy who could not make any attempt at writing. 'A clock is very clever' was another off-the-cuff remark, but the alliteration made it an excellent starting point. Let the children see how you might alter or score out before you think of writing out in best. The final result was written on the round like a clock and all the children in the group contributed their own clock faces to decorate the finished work.

It was included in a large class book and was often used by the children to practise their reading (see photograph on previous page).

As children begin to learn some of the easy phonic sounds it is important to stress that they should always have a go at the initial sound before coming to ask for help. Beginning writing borrows much from the reading curriculum. It should be a mixture of known look-and-say, or look-and-write words e.g. come, house, like, school, play, Superman etc., and words which can be built from some rudimentary knowledge of phonics.

Always encourage children to try out a word, perhaps on a paper slip or using the 'magic line'[*], before asking for help. Encourage use of a wall dictionary, a box dictionary, a list of topic words etc. I do not find individual word books helpful – for a start the teacher has usually to write out the same word thirty times, not just once as for the wall dictionary or topic word list.

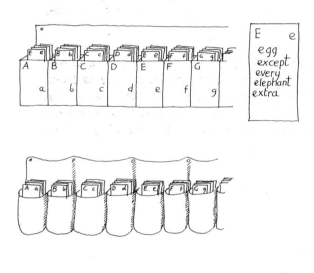

Two ways of making wall dictionaries and an example of topic words in preparation for a visit to the Fire Station

be —— ful (beautiful)
cas —— l (castle)
hos —— tl (hospital)

The 'magic line'

* (The 'magic line' was devised by the National Writing Project. It means that the child who is beginning to try out his writing skills does as much of a word as he can and simply inserts a line where he is unable to complete it. He may want to write the word 'beautiful' but only knows the beginning and the end. He writes 'be-----ful' and this does not interfere with his thought process as he is composing his piece. Advice and corrections come later.)

Beginning writing

It is important to divorce the task of creating or composing from the physical job of making the correct marks in the correct order on paper. Always encourage the children to make a rough copy of their work as soon as they are up and running and have confidence in their ability to write.

The teaching of writing is a very individual business. Children come to it at different times in the school calendar and the infant teacher may have those who are still copying or underwriting in the same class as others who can make a good attempt at a completed poem or coherent story. Work that is a breakthrough for one child could be something of very poor quality for another. More than anything else, children need a great deal of encouragement in their efforts at writing. Getting words on to paper is an enormous undertaking and deserves our congratulations.

THE WRITING ENVIRONMENT
Teachers can create an environment conducive to writing by providing time and space for writing and a variety of easily accessible writing tools.

Space to write. If possible, there should be an area where quiet reigns so that writing is made easy. It should be furnished with tables, chairs and materials, including dictionaries and a wall dictionary.

Time to write. Children in the primary school should be allowed time to work through a piece of writing from first thoughts to completed work. This may mean that a rough draft has to be finished the following day when eye and hand are fresh again.

Tools for writing. Children may wish to make choices about the tools they use for a particular piece of writing, especially as they progress up the school. Pens, pencils, coloured pencils, wax crayons, felt-tips etc. should be made available. For the youngest the pencils and the coloured pencils should be kept sharpened so that no time is wasted. Paper should be available in variety. Use computer paper, the back of hymn sheets etc. for rough work. Keep a variety of coloured and white paper for best work; paste, foil, string, staples, scissors etc. for book-making or final presentation.

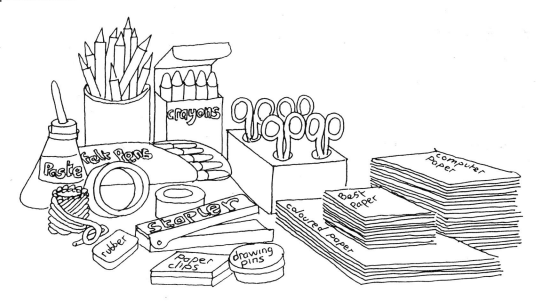

A safe trimmer should be available for older children. Many children, from the infants onwards, may wish to use the jumbo typewriter or word processor.

The writing climate. To provide a working climate for writing, teachers of infants should be ready to act as secretary and to accept children's first independent efforts.

Beginning writing

As children become more skilled and confident, teachers must be able to help them through the problems of drafting and editing. We should encourage them to see writing as a worthwhile activity and should be ready to offer congratulations when work is carried through to a satisfactory conclusion.

The process of writing. Children learn writing at their own pace. They will move themselves on from the use of wax crayons to coloured pencils, to pencils, to pen and ink, and will want to experiment with the word processor.

As they progress, each piece of writing should pass through the stages of starting, composing, revising, editing, publishing (perhaps simply to best work or wall display) and evaluating. Encourage the use of an ideas sheet/mini-thesaurus on rough paper. Do not worry about spelling at this stage. Transfer to composition sheets or rough draft. When this revision stage is completed, the teacher's skill may be required. This is where the *teaching* takes place.

We should allow children the freedom, time and space to develop as writers without fear of constant criticism, and give them an increasing responsibility for their own progress.

This responsibility will vary from classroom to classroom, and indeed from child to child, but, in general, teachers should try to encourage a workshop atmosphere where the children can exchange ideas and criticisms about their own work. In a supportive environment, children will come to see that they have some control over both the process and the product of their writing. They become their own critics and assessors. This leads to a real sense of themselves as authors.

What responsibility can we give children?

They might be allowed to decide:-

- what they will write and when
- whether they prefer paper or exercise books, lined or unlined
- whether to draft in pencil or pen
- which format is most appropriate to their needs
- lists of topics to write about
- when a piece of writing is not worth developing
- to keep a private ideas/writer's notebook
- whether or not to collaborate with others
- to keep examples of work in progress
- whether or not to publish and in what form.

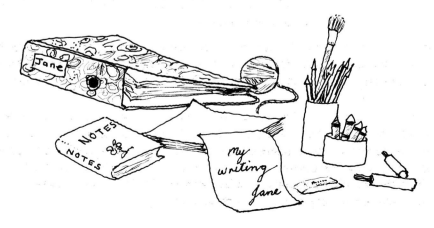

Diaries

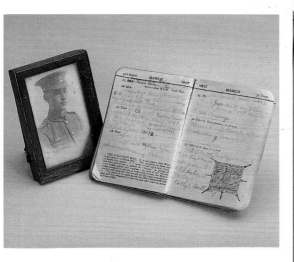

Class display of diary work

True diary-keeping is a very personal affair, not perhaps best suited to the scrutiny of the teacher or the hurly-burly of the classroom. However, diary work can provide a convenient way into the skills of writing in the first person and gives children a strategy for putting direct experience into words.

Discussion. Make a collection of diaries: pocket, kitchen, school-year diaries. Talk about the entries: birthdays to remember, special occasion dates, hairdresser/hospital/dental appointments. Compare these diaries with more personal ones – perhaps from the teacher's own schooldays or a soldier's diary. Look at diaries published in book-form, e.g. *The Country Diary of an Edwardian Lady*, a page from Pepys, *Kilvert's Diary, Adrian Mole* etc. Establish the difference between the impersonal forward-planning diary and more intimate ones.

Diaries

Observation. What can we learn from a diary page from history? What does the following extract tell us about Queen Victoria? It was written when she was a child and still a Princess, on the day her half-sister Feodore and her two children, Eliza and Charles, left Kensington Palace after a visit.

> ** Saturday 26th July 1834*
> *It is such a VERY VERY GREAT HAPPINESS for me to have my DEAREST most DEARLY BELOVED sister with me in my room. . . . . It is TOO DREADFUL for me to think that in an hour I shall not see **Dearest** Feodore's **sweet kind** face, and the **little beauty** Eliza jumping about, and **good honest** Charles running about the room any more. . . . I fell round Feodore's neck and we both cried **bitterly** and pressed each other in our arms **most** tenderly. . . . I sobbed and cried most violently the whole morning.*

* (From 'Queen Victoria's Sketch Book' by Marina Warner, published by Macmillan London Ltd., 1979)

Princess Victoria drew a picture of 'dear little Eliza in her travelling clothes' to accompany this entry.

Talk about the style of writing, the honesty of the young girl's feelings and how reading this piece tells us of her loneliness in the Palace.

Visits. On class outings to museums, libraries and places of interest, e.g. the SS Great Britain in Bristol, encourage the children to look out for personal diaries of famous people – or indeed, the journals kept by ordinary people who happened to be around and wanted to record events. There are diaries of sailors and passengers who went on the first voyage of the SS Great Britain. They record the weather, comment on accommodation and what they had to eat. Get the children to copy a few sentences from historical diaries and make notes (work in groups, so that there is a wide variety of material).

ACTIVITIES

Follow up visits by making diaries. Try to make them look suitably ancient – sewn spines look more authentic than staples. Copy lines from the notes and extend the diaries in imagination, taking on the character of the original writer. Illustrate. This work requires some research and gives practice in the skills of note-taking (see photograph opposite).

Handwriting. Find different ways of making marks on paper. Try to make a quill pen from a feather. Collect as many different writing tools as you can: dip-pens, fountain pens, highlight pens, all thicknesses of pen and pencil. Try coloured inks and coloured pens of all kinds. Make a calligraphy display.

Book-making. Experiment with different size and shape of books. Use a range of colours and types of paper. (This need not be an expensive activity. Many firms are glad to let schools use off-cuts of paper and card.) Try out different ways of collating the pages; sew, staple, glue. Work out the best method for making a personal diary.

History. Copy or photocopy a page or two from diaries across the centuries. Mount and display the pages on a time-line. Illustrate the time-line with the clothes of the period.

Diaries

Diaries written as an historical character – a sailor on the 'H.M.S. Bounty'

Personal diaries. Introduce the children to personal diaries by suggesting that they keep one for a limited time, e.g. for the Easter holidays, for a special event week at school or while they are convalescing in hospital.

Encourage children to make use of their eyes and ears, to write through the senses. Their diaries should be more than simply an extension of the old infant News Books. They should write down, not just what happened, but how they felt about it, what they could see and hear, e.g.

'Me and my friends went to see a play in Marlwood School. We went on a coach. I sat with Johnny. It was called the Pied Piper of Hamelin and it had a Pied Piper there. There was the Mayor and the rats and the King of the Rats. I liked the bit when the Pied Piper got rid of the rats and the Mayor did not give the Pied Piper any money so the Pied Piper took the children away. One of the rats gave us a sweet before we came away.'

This was not the 'best' piece of writing from the class, but this boy has attempted to give a résumé of the story and tells us what he liked best, making it a vivid account of a day in the life of a six-year-old child.

Suggest that children might keep a diary over a restricted period: an Advent diary; diary of my holiday to . . . .; diary of my sister's wedding; diary of my visit to hospital (a very important therapeutic idea).

Diaries

Make the diaries short, so that children can see the end in sight. Let them choose size, shape and colour of paper. Make them very personal, perhaps working out the number of pages required. They could present each page in a different way, outlined and illustrated, perhaps printing day and date in 'illuminated script'.

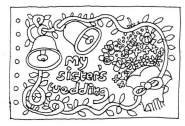

Private diaries. The point about this kind of diary is that it really should be private. It is a diary in which children record their thoughts and feelings, note down things that make them feel happy or sad, scribble down ideas for future stories or poems. Let them use it as a writer's notebook. Some children may wish to bring this diary to the teacher, but she cannot insist. It is a private document and must be respected.

For My Eyes Only! A private diary with a difference. Make this an adventure diary. Plan to storm the Tower of London/thumb a lift on a space ship/fly (in disguise) to Australia/be a stowaway on a pirate ship. Note down your day-to-day plans in your diary. Make a bold illustrated cover. Experiment to find ways of locking it securely. Try pins or paper clips or elastic bands. Make the diary look like a TOP SECRET document. Make a marbled cover, decorate with a seal made from shiny red paper.

Keep Out! This is a private diary used for personal thoughts and feelings. Choose a very fierce animal with snapping teeth to defend your diary: lion, tiger, crocodile. Fold a double page in the middle, colour with felt-tips and cut out as illustrated. Fix the animal head into your book and it will snap at anybody who opens your diary without permission.

Pop-up dog.
you need 2 sheets of paper, 1side 3 times longer than the other.

Keep Out!

Diaries

Class diary kept over an extended period of time

Garden diary. This diary works best as a group project. Make it quite large (A3 perhaps) and arrange it month by month through the school year. Children who take part in the digging, planting, weeding etc. should record progress perhaps using diagrams. Paste in seed packets and note date of sowing. Observe the growth of plants and seedlings and record. Note the birds and insects who visit the garden. Paste in individual entries and illustrations, scrap-book fashion (see photograph).

Pond diary. Another group diary organised as above. Show the progress of work required to keep the pond in good shape. Observe and record the growth and transformation of pond creatures, water plants and visiting insects. Make this a round diary in the shape of a pond. On the cover, use torn tissue paper, pasted flat, to make weeds; pond creatures with felt-tip pens or shiny paper; colour the pond itself in oil-based pastel or wax crayon. Overlay with a see-through cover using an overhead projector transparency sheet.

Use diluted Indian inks to make background for the pond diary cover, and overlay with cut-out, ink-painted dragonfly, rushes etc. (see cover of *Words with Wings*). Garden and pond diaries give practice in observational/scientific writing.

Concertina Diaries. Concertina diaries are an excellent way of tackling life-story sequences, e.g. butterfly/frog/apple tree/dandelion seed. Use thin card and work a page at a time. Note each stage in the life cycle in words and pictures. Use a different medium for each page: wax resist, pencil crayon, collage, paint. When the pages are completed assemble the diary lengthways, taping the pages at the back so that it can stand open, perhaps at the back of a nature table display. This kind of diary can also be used to show the migration pattern of swallows/geese/house martins.

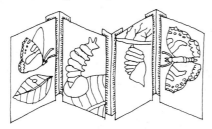

Diary Poems. Either use the private diary as a starter, letting the children choose a sentence or a phrase from which to start or, better still, go outside and look and listen. Make notes. Put the ideas together watching the rhythm and build into a poem. You can use the date as a title.

> **Three days into March**
>
> Today
>   the birds sang
> and yellow crocuses
> opened wide their mouths
>   to feast on
>   sunlight.
>
> Today
>   the sky cleared
> and enthusiastic trees
> stretched out their limbs
>   all thick with
>   promises
>
> Today
>   I stood still
> and the greens, the blues
> and the yellows clamoured
>   to dance behind
>   my eyes.
>
> **Moira Andrew**

School Diary. Make a diary showing the public events throughout the school year. Work as a group, on the scrap book principle. Use photographs, programmes, invitations etc. in addition to text and illustrations. Groups of top infants or lower juniors could make these diaries for new pupils and their parents. They could read and present the diaries on preparation days for beginners. They should tell not only what happens in school during the year, but how it feels to take part in these events.

Diaries

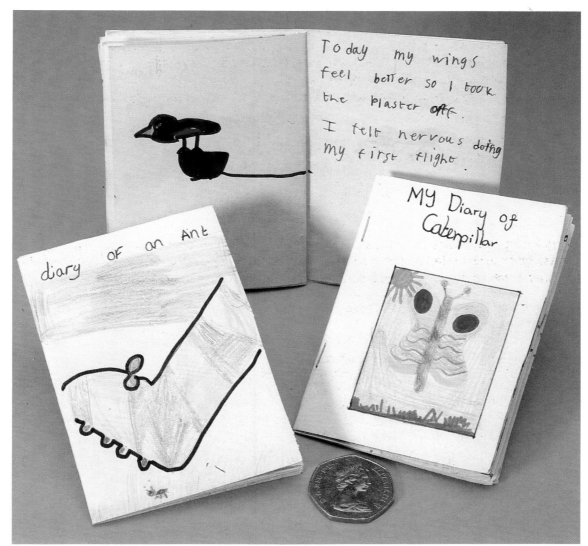

To day my wings feel better so I took the plaster off.
I felt nervous doing my first flight.

diary of an Ant

MY Diary of Caterpillar

Mini-diaries for tiny creatures

Mini-Diary. Make a very small diary for a tiny creature. Pretend that you are that creature and work your way through a week. You might like to read Eric Carle's story *A Very Hungry Caterpillar* first. For the youngest children suggest that each page begins simply 'On Monday . . .', 'On Tuesday . . .' and so on. Think about how the small creature (worm, bird, caterpillar, mouse, ladybird) might feel. Look at the way Christopher in his bird diary writes 'I felt really nervous doing my first flight. It felt marvellous when I was really flying. I saw houses underneath and trees looking like matchsticks.' He is really thinking about how he would feel if he were a bird (see photograph above).

Diaries from Published Books. Use published diaries as a starter. Look at *The Country Diary of an Edwardian Lady*. Go out on a country walk. Take a notebook. Note down what you see and hear. Make sketches of the wild flowers. Put your walk into diary form as in the Edwardian Lady. Use brown ink and best handwriting. Add painted sketches of flowers (see display photograph). Published diaries could follow the 'What happened next?' technique. What happened when the Edwardian lady was late home? What happened when she got paint on her dress? How did her diaries get lost and found?

Diaries

Diaries from long ago. Collect some old diaries if possible. Read snippets from the pages to get some idea of what the writer's life was like (see Discussion and Observation). Let the children choose a piece that appeals to them. Make a diary similar in size and shape to the original. Cut out the sentence that was of interest and continue the diary as if you were the writer. Watch that details of dress, food, artefacts are more or less of the period. This gives good practice in the skills of research. Illustrate.

Here is an extract from a soldier's diary. Look at the date (see photograph on page 11).

> *Sunday 11th February 1917*
> Church Parade. Guard duty. Answered Dad's and Harold's letters.
>
> *Monday 12th February 1917*
> Flooded out of guard tent. Cleaned up for OC inspection. Paraded in greatcoats.
>
> *Tuesday 13th February, 1917*
> Route march. 1/2 day washing. To go for photographs this evening. Remember Aunt Dora's birthday.
>
> *Wednesday 14th February 1917*
> Swedish drill. Short route march. 1/2 day football match – Med. Staff 1, RAMC 0.

Why do you think that the soldier wrote in such short phrases, note-fashion? What were the highlights of his week? Where do you think that he was at the time? What do you think might happen next? Write a continuation of his diary for the following week. Make your diary small (pocket-sized) and very battered-looking. Write in note form.

Take one day. Record one day in the life of Father/Mother Christmas/Batman/Noah/St. Francis of Assisi etc. Choose a character from history or from fiction. Look at books about the historical character. Make notes about a typical day. Write as if you were that person.

Make diary in a suitable shape e.g. pot of honey for Pooh Bear, Batman mask for Batman, the ark for Noah. Write and illustrate all the routine or interesting facts that happened during one day. Tell about the weather, what they had to eat, what they said.

Letters

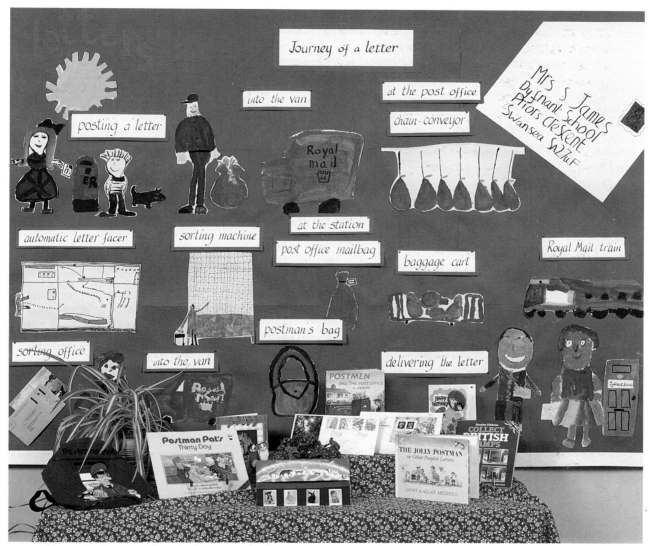

Class display showing the journey of a letter

Letters connect writer and reader in a very direct way. There are many people who may never write a poem or a story after leaving school, but everyone writes letters; notes to the milkman, 'Thank You' notes, an exchange of family news, the formal letter to those in high places. Because letters conform to a pattern and one letter usually leads to another in reply, most children enjoy letter-writing, especially when this is presented as a real-life task and there is an obvious purpose to the work.

Discussion. Make a collection of the letters received during one week. Ask the children to contribute (where appropriate). There will be gas bills, letters from the bank, newsletters about forthcoming events, personal letters. There may be birthday cards or invitations. Try and acquire a cross section from postcards to formal typewritten business letters. Look at how they are produced: handwritten, typewritten, word-processed. Talk about the purpose of each kind of letter, why it was written, language used and the kind of reply required. Sort the letters into groups.

Arrange to have the Post Office educational pack delivered. Look at the history behind the present day Post Office: uniforms, ways of delivery, stamps. Find out about its origins. Look at stamp collections. Make a collection of foreign stamps.

Letters

Visits. Make a visit to the local Post Office. Talk to the postmen. Ask about their 'walks'. Make a graph/map of the different areas each postman covers. Visit the sorting office. Find out how letters are sorted, the way postcodes are used, how letters travel to different locations. Post a letter to your own class. Find out about the stages it goes through on its journey from pillar box to delivery at school.

ACTIVITIES

Look for examples of letters in history books. Find out as much as you can about the writers. Make copies of the letters and write a reply keeping to the appropriate style and language of the period. Illustrate.

Learn how to set out a letter correctly. Use your post code or that of the school. Have a class competition to see who can produce the neatest piece of work when everybody simply copies a short letter.

Danescourt Junior School
Danescourt Way
LLandaff
Cardiff
CF5 2RB

Dear Mrs Gordon
We are making lots of books in school. We have made some picture books to help little children with their reading. The children have to lift a flap to find out who is hiding underneath. We think they will enjoy this.

Could you help show us how you put your books together? Please come and visit Danescourt School soon.

love from
Lucy, Rachel and Samantha

Get to know a class of children in a school in a different setting from your own. Exchange letters and photographs, newsletters and paintings. You may be able to have a pen friend in the other school. It could be a very interesting occasion if a class from an urban school follows up the correspondence by visiting children in a rural area. It might also be possible to write to children in schools in another country. Use your letters to find out how other people live, what the weather is like, what clothes they wear etc. Make a book about your own school and send it to your opposite number.

Letters

Design a wildlife stamp

Designs for postage stamps

Design a wildlife stamp

Design a stamp. Design a stamp to commemorate a special occasion. Make wildlife stamps, stamps of famous buildings, sports stamps, Christmas stamps. Use wax crayons, felt-tip pens or paint. Make the stamps about A4 size. Have a competition. Make a collage of the finished designs (see photograph).

Handwriting. Look at letters from the 19th century or early years of the 20th century. Look at the way handwriting has changed. Rule some pages in thick and thin lines and practise copperplate writing. Write a letter to an elderly person in your best copperplate asking what school was like when they went to school.

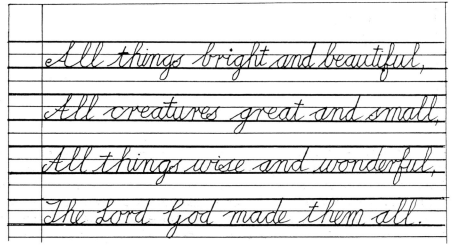

All things bright and beautiful,
All creatures great and small,
All things wise and wonderful,
The Lord God made them all.

Copperplate writing

Letters

Letters to newspapers: If there is something that worries you about your local environment, think very hard about it and make notes about why it is so disturbing. Perhaps the Council intends to close a wildlife area, run a motorway across your village, knock down an old building, fell some very ancient trees to make way for a supermarket. Try to find out the facts behind the story, when it is to happen and why. Assemble your facts and suggest suitable alternatives, then put them together into a polite letter to your local newspaper. Do a first draft, correct spelling and punctuation and write it out in best. Make sure that you set out your letter correctly. Find out the correct address of the editor from the paper. Keep a copy of your letter and make a display of the problem, your letter and any reply you receive. Write also to the appropriate councillor involved.

Work as a group and think of things that would make your village/town a better place to live in: less litter, a safe playground for pre-school children, a scented garden for blind people, a nature/urban trail, safer pavement surfaces for older people etc. Make notes, consider your reasons, suggest the best place to start, say whether you think children might be able to help in the planning. Plan the form of your letter together. Check spelling and punctuation. Ask the neatest person in the group to write the letter or put it on the word-processor. Follow the progress of your suggestion and keep copies of all the letters.

Letters to writers, artists and other school visitors. Find the addresses of local writers, artists and musicians from the local Regional Arts Association. Write a letter to someone whose work interests you. Ask where their ideas come from, how they work best, what materials they like to use etc. If the writer has visited the school send a letter of thanks, say what you liked best (or didn't like) about the visit and send a copy of some of the follow-up work you have done.

Special occasion cards. Design your own Mother's Day, Easter, Christmas, birthday cards. Look at professional examples and find out how the greetings are usually worded. Write your own greeting inside the card and send it off.

Special occasion cards

Letters

Postcards. Design a postcard for your own area. Make it the same size and shape as a bought card. Rule a space for the address and the stamp on the back and write out a short message telling what you have been doing that day. You have to be very careful to use only a few words, so think carefully before you write the card. Send the card off to a pen friend, your grandparents, a friend who lives some distance away or to children in another school.

Dear Giovanni
This is a postcard of my school. You can see my house, no.17. I am the girl who is skipping. I am 8 years old. I like riding my bicycle, reading and playing the piano. I also like listening to pop records. I will look forward to a letter from you
yours sincerely Betty Cook.

Giovanni Angelino
Pierra della Francesca street
Sienna
Tuscany
Italy

Letters for information. You may want to find out about what a museum/place of historical interest can offer your school. You may want to find out whether a particular brand of soap powder/ cleaner/hair spray etc. is as 'green' as it might be. You may want to find out about children's events in your area in the holidays. Find the name and address of the person in charge and set out your questions in a polite and ordered way.

Dear Me. Write a letter addressed to yourself at forty, fifty, sixty. Tell all that you have done today, the people you have played with, the work you have been doing in school, what you had for lunch, what the weather is like, what you are wearing. Tell a little of what is in today's news. Remember that you will forget the details in time to come, so make your letter very detailed. Illustrate. Put the sealed letter away in a safe place and don't be tempted to open it.

Dear Weather. Write a letter to the sun/wind/snow/rain asking why it behaves as it does. Make this a very imaginative letter saying how you feel about each kind of weather. Follow the pattern of a real-life letter. Arrange the finished letters on a weather frieze.

Letters from history. Choose a character from history: Mary, Queen of Scots, Guy Fawkes, King Alfred, Florence Nightingale etc. Find out as much as you can about the person from books. Write a letter as though you were that person e.g. Florence Nightingale to her mother back home; Mary, mother of Jesus, to the innkeeper's wife; King Arthur to one of his knights etc.

Letters

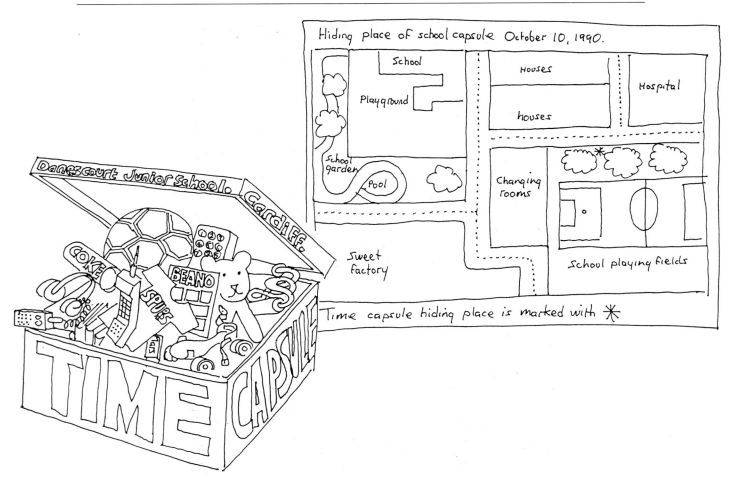

Hiding place of school capsule October 10, 1990.

School · Houses · Hospital · Playground · houses · School garden · Pool · Changing rooms · Sweet factory · School playing fields

Time capsule hiding place is marked with ✳

Danescourt Junior School. Cardiff

Time Capsule. Think of a few things which you can collect which will give a flavour of what life is like for children at school today. You might choose a small toy, a crisp or biscuit wrapper, a school photograph, a list of class names, a page of a newspaper etc. Write some letters to the children of the future, each person in the group choosing a different topic to write about e.g. a new invention, today's headline, a synopsis of a favourite story/film/video, the most popular television programme, today's fashion, what is happening at school, portraits of the teachers etc. Illustrate. Put all the things in a sealed airtight tin and bury it in a corner of the school field. Mark the place on a plan of the school. Date it.

Father Christmas letters. Christmas gives the youngest infants the ideal opportunity for letter-writing – every child enjoys writing to Father Christmas listing her wishes. Encourage the children to go a stage further and ask questions, e.g. How cold is it at the North Pole? What are you having for Christmas dinner? How is Mother Christmas keeping? Post the letters in a special post box and let the Top Juniors write replies as Father/Mother Christmas characters. (Read J.R.R. Tolkien's *The Father Christmas Letters*, Allen & Unwin, and enjoy turning the tables!)

'The Jolly Postman'. Read Allan Ahlberg's *The Jolly Postman* (published by Heinemann). Make your own book in the Allan Ahlberg style. Put pockets on every other page to fit all the different kinds of letter which the postman might deliver to your door. Use ideas from the characters in nursery rhymes and fables e.g. a Get Well card to Red Riding Hood's granny; an invitation asking the Ugly Sisters to the Royal Ball; an angry letter from the Troll to the Three Billy Goats Gruff telling them to keep off the Rickety-Rackety Bridge; a birth congratulations card to the parents of Baby Bunting; a birthday card from Goldilocks to Baby Bear. Make this a group project.

Invitations

Collage display of invitations: paint and wet paper background with oil-based pastel cut-outs

Invitations usually mean an exciting event coming soon, so children enjoy thinking about this kind of writing. The essence of the writing required for invitations is that it should convey all the necessary information in very few words. Invitations impose their own economy on the writer.

Discussion. Make a collection of invitations to as many events as possible; weddings, parties, school occasions etc. Look at the kind of information they contain, and make a list of the most commonly used words; days of the week, times of the day, months. (This is a good way of helping children to become familiar with the sequence and spelling of days and months.)

Encourage the children to write their own invitations where possible. This kind of activity makes the work quite personal and provides the children with an opportunity to write with purpose.

ACTIVITIES
Artists, writers, musicians. When the school is holding a Book Week, Arts Festival or Master Class, let the children write to artists, writers and musicians whose work they enjoy. Invite the artists to school suggesting suitable dates and giving an indication of what might take place during the visit. The invitations could be illustrated. (These would usually require a covering letter confirming the invitation, offering a fee etc.)

Invitations

Please come
to our Hallowe'en
Party

At the school,
Friday, 12 oct. 8pm.
Fancy dress

Please come to
our nativity
play

At the school
16th December,
Wednesday
at 6 pm.

Invitations to school events

School Events. Let the children write invitations to parents/Senior Citizens/advisers etc. to the various events held in school. Fold thin card or drawing paper and cut into a suitable shape which suggests what is to take place e.g. apple for Harvest Thanksgiving, mask for the Hallowe'en party, star/stable/crown for the Nativity play, strawberry for the Strawberry Tea. Colour and decorate the cover. Write the invitation inside. Neatness and correct spelling are important.

Parental/Community help. Where the class would like help with a project e.g. history, gardening, baking etc. the children can write their own invitations to parents and members of the community.

Party invitations. Use thin card, folded. Make party invitations for your own birthday party. Note what information your guests will need, then write it all out neatly using felt-tip pen. Decorate the cards using felt-tip pen or collage. Invite your friends to a 'bouncy' party, a burger party, a fancy dress party and make invitations to suit. Put up a party display using balloons, party poppers and streamers (see photograph).

Invitations can also be used for imaginary or fantastic events.

Dear Mickey Mouse. Make up an invitation to your favourite cartoon character inviting him to a party on the moon/under the sea/on a magic carpet/in a rain forest. Be sure to give time and date and clear instructions to the place where the party is to be held.

To Florence Nightingale/Alfred the Great. Invite your favourite character from history to visit you at home. Suggest that it might be rather different from what the world was like in their day. Suggest what they should wear, what food to expect, how to find your house. (Put a map inside your invitation.) Illustrate.

Party Invitations (see facing page)

The Ugly Bug Ball. Listen to the tape of Rolf Harris singing 'The Ugly Bug Ball'. Write out a suitable invitation to the ball. Invent your own 'Ugly Bugs' using paint, felt-tip pens or oil-based crayons. Make them funny, fantastic, foolish. Cut out the individual bugs and paste on to a night-time forest frieze. Place the invitation on the picture (see display photograph).

Cinderella. Write an invitation asking Cinderella to come to the Ball. The invitation will have come from a Royal Prince, so it will be very grand. Give time, place and date. Suggest the kind of clothes Cinderella should wear, e.g. 'Ball gowns will be worn.' Decorate the invitation with gold or silver pen.

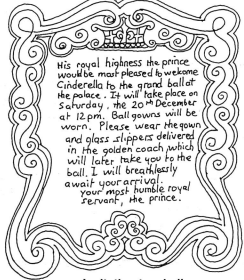

Invitation to a ball

Recipes

Recipes are written to a formula. The ability to set down instructions in such a way that others can follow them is an important skill for children to learn. Working on the recipe form is one way of coming to terms with this discipline. The bonus of following a recipe to its logical conclusion and eating the results has an added attraction for most children!

Discussion. Make a collection of cookery books. Look at the way a recipe is set out, usually listing the ingredients, then giving method and preparation time. Talk about favourite recipes. Make a graph of food likes and dislikes. Talk about healthy eating and the need for hygiene in the kitchen.

Look for recipes for both sweets and savouries. Talk about what makes things taste sweet/salty/sour/bitter. Organise a tasting session. Get the children to work blindfolded. Taste and guess apple/pear/raw potato, cinnamon/ginger/sugar/salt, lemon/orange/grapefruit etc.

Visits. Visit the school kitchen. Copy out the day's menu. Watch the cook at work. Find out if she has had to adjust the recipes to suit the number of children taking school lunch on that day. Ask about any unusual words and phrases used in the recipes, e.g. blend, simmer, bake blind, and find out what they mean. (Copy out some of the recipes and later work out the amounts needed for your own family.)

Visit the local bakery. Note all the ingredients needed to bake bread. Watch and note the process. Look at the deft movements of the baker as he kneads the dough, shapes it, puts it in the oven. Watch how the dough rises. Smell the new bread as it is taken from the oven. Look at the different shapes/colour/texture of the loaves. Taste the new bread.

ACTIVITIES

Cooking sessions. Find and write out some simple recipes which can be made in school. Enlist the help of parents and run cooking/baking sessions. Encourage the children to weigh, mix, wash up etc. on their own.

Recipes from other countries. Make a collection of recipes from other countries. Encourage children from different ethnic backgrounds to talk about foods typical of their own culture. Ask parents to share recipes and show how special dishes are prepared and served.

National day. Have an Indian/Chinese/Welsh/Scottish day and prepare an appropriate menu. Display the recipes around the walls. Make recipe books. Invite parents and members of the local community as guests. Let them try some of the special dishes on offer. Encourage the children to tell how they are made. Sell the recipe books and donate the proceeds to a charity which cares for those who don't have enough to eat.

Traditional recipes. Copy a traditional/family/ethnic easy-to-make recipe on a large sheet. Use paint or oil-based pastels for the individual ingredients and kitchen utensils needed. Cut out and paste on a wall frieze around the recipe. Assemble books and materials relating to the recipe on a table below (see display photograph).

welsh leek soup.

5 potatoes
4 leeks
1 onion
2 eggs
butter
Flour
cream

Flour
butter
cream

Class display of recipe work: painted collage with ingredients and Dolly Brown's cakes

My Best Things. Get children to make individual books of their own ten favourite recipes. Copy the recipe form carefully. Illustrate.

Old family recipes. Ask parents and grandparents for old recipes which have been handed down to the family. Find out about the background and make notes. Assemble the recipes, notes about the family history, kitchen utensils used etc. Illustrate and add old photographs, if possible. Collect together in a class book. (See 'Dolly Brown's Louise Cakes' in the display photograph.)

Recipes

Healthy Eating. Talk to the school nurse or invite the dietician from the local hospital. Find out about healthy eating and put together a book of recommended recipes and suggestions for lunch boxes and picnics.

Harvest Thanksgiving. Find bread-making recipes. Work in groups and make bread using different kinds of flour: strong white/wholegrain/wheatmeal. Make the loaves in different shapes. Arrange on the Harvest table. You could also make butter from the top of the milk, and jam from berries collected from the hedgerows to go with the bread. Display the recipes on a board behind the Harvest table.

Bread and Water. Older children might like to organise a bread and water day, using the bread recipes which they have collected. For one day only children, parents and teachers eat a lunch of bread (as much as you like) with water to drink and perhaps a piece of fruit to follow. The lunch money saved is collected and sent to a famine-relief charity.

Sweets for Christmas. Make a collection of non-cook sweet recipes. There are lots of them. Make a class book in the shape of a toffee. Write out and illustrate the recipes. Make a selection of the sweets (peppermints, coconut ice, peanut treats, chocolate fudge bars etc.). Cut into shapes and wrap individually. Put one or two of each variety into small plastic food bags and make bright Christmas labels. Give to children in the local hospital or to senior citizens at Christmas time.

Hallowe'en, Bonfire, Christmas cakes. Design a pattern for icing the top of a cake for a special occasion. Suggest a green face for Hallowe'en, a snow scene for Christmas, red and yellow firework patterns for Bonfire Night etc.

Unusual recipes. Look for recipes which tell you how to make paper, pot-pourri, invisible ink. Try out the recipes and see if they work. Then make up your own recipe for something which has never before appeared in a cookery book, e.g. a recipe for a playground game, planting seeds, making a mask etc.

Recipe to make my dad, brother, sister, grandma MAD! Think of something you do which makes your family cross.

Ingredients
One boy called Sam, a large muddy puddle, a pair of new shoes, a very wet afternoon.
Method
Put two new shoes on a boy called Sam. Take him outside on a very wet afternoon. Find a large muddy puddle and mix all the ingredients, stirring well.
Preparation time
Two minutes to make a mother truly MAD!
(This recipe *never* fails!)

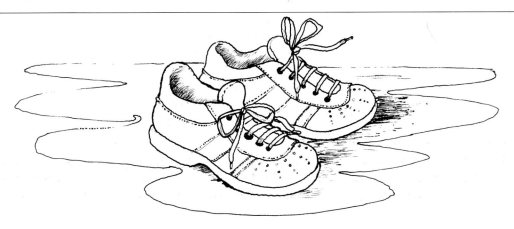

Recipe to turn my teacher into a toad.
Imagine you are a witch/wizard. Write out a spell to turn your teacher into a toad! Make it like a recipe: list your ingredients, method and preparation time. You can be as funny or outrageous as you like, but you must stick to the recipe formula.

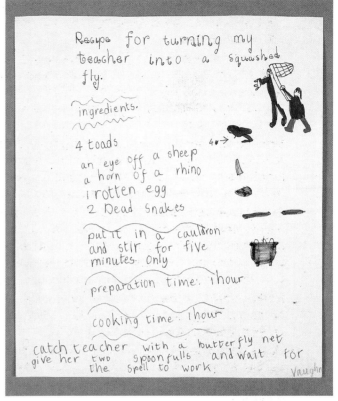

Recipe for a sand castle. Using the recipe form, write out what you need to build a sandcastle (ingredients), how you would go about it (method), and how long you think it will take (preparation time). Use the same idea to write out how to build a snowman or a miniature garden, make a leaf/bark rubbing or a woolly pom-pom.

Recipe for a Greener World. Look at magazines which are concerned with conservation, the rainforests, pollution. Work with a group and pool your ideas to make the world a greener place. Put them together in recipe form and make a colourful wall display.

Recipe for a happy day. List all the ingredients you think you need to make a really wonderful day. Use your imagination to make them into a recipe, e.g.

Recipe for happiness

Take a slice of sunshine
Add a pinch of breeze
Stir in a jug of birdsong
Mix them as you please
Allow one afternoon
with nothing to do
        but daydream.

Moira Andrew

The Ugly Duckling. Read Hans Andersen's story of the Ugly Duckling who was so sad and upset when he saw himself reflected in the lake. He thought he was the ugliest thing he had ever seen. Make up a spell to turn the Ugly Duckling into a beautiful swan. Write it out in recipe form.

Prayers

Most children will be familiar with the formal prayers used in assembly or in their own church. When children are given the opportunity to think about and write prayers for themselves, they have a deep sense of involvement and are able to practise their writing skills with purpose.

In our multi-faith society, it is important that children are introduced to religions other than their own. Making up prayers is an excellent way-in to thinking about how different people worship. The children can follow a calendar of religious festivals over the school year. They can make up their own prayers of thanks and entreaty, of hope and love – each written to suit the occasion.

Some of the children's prayers will be public, intended for reading aloud at assembly or for display in book form or on the wall, but others should be accepted as utterly private, neither to be shared nor corrected.

Discussion. Talk about how prayers, both public and private, are used. Find out if children know any prayers off by heart e.g. The Lord's Prayer, and 'Thank You for the world so sweet'. Let the others join in. Talk about who usually leads others in prayer. Talk about the times of day when prayers are offered e.g. Morning Assembly, Evensong, Muslim midday prayers. Let Jewish/Chinese/Hindu/Muslim children share their customs with the others. Discuss special times of the year when religious festivals take place e.g. Christmas, Easter, Chinese New Year, Ramadan, Diwali (the Festival of Lights).

Visits. Arrange a visit to the local church, mosque, temple, chapel or synagogue. Look at the way in which prayers are presented e.g. on scrolls as in the Jewish Torah; in elaborate calligraphy as inside a mosque; in a Prayer Book as in the Church of England. Talk to the priest in charge and ask if there is a hidden place where written prayers can be found. Look for special prayers like those written by St. Francis of Assisi.

ACTIVITIES

Christmas. Write prayers of thanks for the joys that Christmas brings. Write them on strips of yellow paper and assemble as rays round a huge gold star pasted on to a dark background. You could place the star of prayer above a nativity scene.

Young tree with children's prayers displayed on torn tissue paper strips

Prayer Tree. You might like to write prayers on long strips of the finest paper that you can find which allows you to write without tearing. Mount the prayers on strips of coloured tissue paper. If you can get hold of a broken branch or a young tree still in its pot, tie your prayers to the branches and set up the prayer tree on a display table. Decorate the background with symbols of different religions and place holy books or statues around it. This would be a lovely way to pray for a friend who is ill or has met with an accident. Paint a picture of the prayer tree or take its photograph and send it to your friend in hospital. He or she will know that they haven't been forgotten (see display photograph).

Make a collection of books about different religions. Make a calendar of religious festivals and display it on the classroom wall. It may be possible to borrow religious artefacts from different religions to make a display corner. Ask children to write prayers to be used in the displays.

Prayers

Diwali, Festival of Lights. In their Festival of Lights, Hindus celebrate the triumph of good over evil. Make up prayers of thanks for all the lights in the world; candlelight, sunlight, starlight, moonlight. Think how dark and dreary life would be without light. Think of all the lights we use at home and the electricity which powers them. Think of the lights which save lives e.g. lighthouse, traffic lights. Think of all the lights which make us happy: fireworks, bonfires, Christmas lights. Arrange your prayers about lights in candle shapes and display them with examples of other kinds of lights: lamps, torches, lanterns etc. Use lots of yellow and gold and make a display to celebrate light in the world.

Prayer Wheel. Some Buddhist shrines have prayer wheels. These are made from a wooden drum with paper fixed to the outside. A mantra or prayer is written on the paper. It can be read on the round. Write prayers of thanks for mountains and water and flowers and mount them on a prayer wheel.

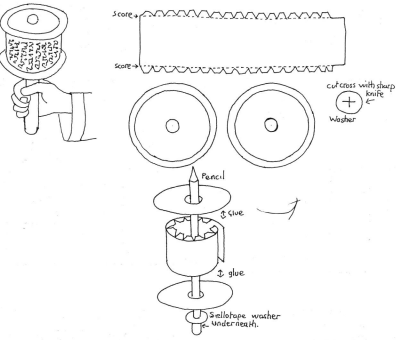

Harvest Thanksgiving. Work in groups. Think of all the different things that are grown and harvested in order to feed us. Think of the food which is free. Think of the food which has to be gathered from the sea. Think of those who do not have enough to eat. Make up prayers of thanks for the food from farms and orchards, from hedgerows, from the sea. Make prayers for those who do not have enough food for themselves or for their children. Make prayer banners to hang in the hall at the Harvest Festival. Make prayers to fit into books shaped like apples, fish, loaves and vegetables. You might be able to collect donations of money at the end of the service. These could be sent with your prayers to organisations who help feed the hungry children of the world e.g. Save the Children Fund. Take the food collected for the Harvest Table to Senior Citizens' homes, hospitals etc. Put a copy of a harvest prayer inside each parcel.

Id al-Fitr, the Festival of Fast-breaking. This is a Muslim festival which marks the end of Ramadan. Muslims listen to special prayers and have new clothes. They eat special foods and sweets. Families and friends visit one another. They give enough money to buy a meal for the poorest people in their town. You could make up prayers to show that you are thinking about people who do not have enough to eat or warm clothes to wear. You could make sweets from coconut and sweetened milk. Wrap the sweets in bright paper on which you have written your prayers for the poor people. Share the sweets with your friends.

Prayers

Prayer Scroll. Find a picture of the Jewish Torah. These are scrolls which are very holy. Make a scroll from wooden dowels and glue a long piece of paper to each, so that it can be rolled up like an ancient book or scroll. Decorate the top of the dowel with the picture of a lion or an eagle or a crown. (Use felt-tip pens and draw the symbol on a folded sheet of paper so that you have two matching shapes when it is cut out. Colour both sides and glue over the top of the wooden dowel.) Write class prayers to be read from the prayer scroll as it is unrolled. Make them very colourful as the Torah scrolls are usually richly decorated.

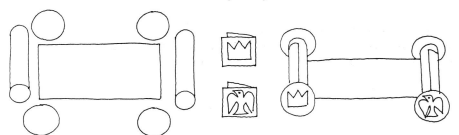

Cut 4 cardboard discs slightly larger than ends of dowels. Fold 2 pieces of coloured paper in half, to cut 2 crowns and 2 eagles. Glue these to the ends of dowels. Glue ends of paper on to each dowel as in drawings.

Yuan Tan, Chinese New Year's Day. The Chinese New Year is at the end of January and is celebrated with fireworks and lanterns. Write prayers on lantern shapes which can be opened to reveal the prayers. String them from the walls.

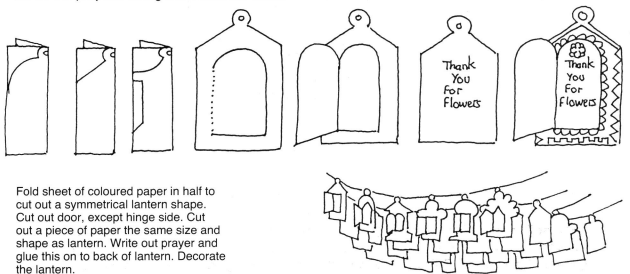

Fold sheet of coloured paper in half to cut out a symmetrical lantern shape. Cut out door, except hinge side. Cut out a piece of paper the same size and shape as lantern. Write out prayer and glue this on to back of lantern. Decorate the lantern.

Easter. Make Easter cards to celebrate the day that Jesus rose again. You can write prayers of thanks for springtime and all the new growth in the fields and gardens. Write your prayer carefully inside the Easter card and take it home to surprise your parents on Easter morning.

Plainsong. Monks make up prayers from texts in the Bible and sing them in church. Find a verse or a phrase from the Bible and make it into a simple prayer. Make up a tune to accompany it using percussion instruments. At the next assembly, sing your prayers to your own tune as monks used to do with plainsong.

Prayer Dance. Although prayers are usually written down, or at least put into words, it is easily forgotten than you can dance a prayer. Make up a simple prayer, perhaps one which gives thanks for the lovely things in our world: waves on the sea; trees which sway in the breeze; leaves which dance down to earth in autumn; snow which falls softly in winter; rain which nourishes all growing things. Now put your prayer into movement and dance a prayer of thanksgiving at the next assembly.

Posters

Children are very familiar with the concept of the poster. We (and they!) are bombarded at every turn by hoardings, press and television advertising. We are exhorted to buy everything from boots to boats, sweets to sweaters. We are encouraged to attend events in school, in church, at the cinema, theatre and art gallery. We are invited to save the environment, pick up litter, give to charity. The poster is perhaps the most public way of using words. Children often know the slogans that advertisers use, and know that a simple message is necessary, often accompanied by an eye-catching visual.

Discussion. Talk about the places where posters are to be found. Why are posters sited in such prominent places? Why are larger-than-life letters used? What are posters trying to do? Look at a selection of posters urging us to buy, to attend a function, to give, to think about the environment. Organise a group guessing game where the punch line is read aloud and the others have to guess the product. Look at the unusual way advertisers use words.

Make a display of posters, one half commercial materials, the other your own version of the same posters.

Visits. It may be possible to visit a design studio where poster artwork is carried out. Look at the stages through which a design goes, from ideas to rough to final work. Take some of the best ideas for a poster from the class as it is possible that the studio will make up a poster to show the process.

ACTIVITIES

Design a machine. Suggest that the children work in groups to design a machine that would make the environment better, e.g. a garbage gobbler, a pedal-powered car, a CFC vacuum cleaner etc. the more zany the better. Get together to produce a design, decide who would benefit from such a device and then make advertisements to persuade people to buy it. This activity would fit in with the design and technology curriculum.

School events. Design and print posters to encourage parents and friends to attend the Christmas performance, the Summer Fete, the Jumble Sale, the annual Sports Day etc. Make sure that you include date and time of the event, admission price, if necessary. Make the lettering an important part of the poster so that it appears uncluttered. Correct spelling and neatness are also important. Illustrate with an appropriate picture. Discuss where your posters would be displayed to best advantage so that they are read by your 'target audience', i.e. the people who would be most likely to attend the event.

Save the Environment posters

Save the Environment. Discuss the environmental issues of endangered animals, threatened rainforests etc. and work in groups to design and prepare posters to encourage people to think about these problems. Read literature prepared by Friends of the Earth, Greenpeace etc. Pick out an animal or area of the world in which you are interested and design a 'Save the Whale, Otter, Badger, Rainforest . . .' etc. poster. Make sure that your poster gives enough information to make people think about the issue. Make sure it is eye-catching, sad, beautiful, funny (see display photograph).

Litterbug Monsters. Decide what a Litterbug Monster would look like. Would he have green teeth? a Coke can body? bottle legs? hair made from chocolate wrappers? Make a Litterbug Monster from junk. Write an anti-litter slogan to put below your Litterbug.

Wayside Pulpit. Look at the posters that you can see outside churches. Find out from the Head Teacher what the assemblies are to be about for the next week or two. Make posters to advertise each assembly. Letter the text or message carefully and paint a picture to go along with it. Pin the posters in the hall and corridor.

Sing-a-Jingle. Make up a jingle to sell your favourite sweets/soft drink. It must be simple, use few words well and it should rhyme. It should be catchy and easy to remember. Make up a tune to go with it and play it on percussion instruments.

Posters

Book News. When you write your own book (see Book section), design a poster to encourage people to read it. Give the title and the author's name. Say whether it is a book for young children, an adventure story, a comic book or whatever. Make the poster so exciting that people would want to rush out and buy your book.

Design a T-shirt. Many of us wear posters. Look at the T-shirts you see people wearing. Design a logo to print on the front of a T-shirt. It should have a simple message, e.g. Save the Trees, Fragile Earth, etc. You might design a T-shirt for your school with the name of the school and a suitable illustration. It is possible to have these designs printed on to plain white T-shirts.

Design a carrier bag. Many stores have mini-posters in the form of bags which the customers carry about with them. Design a bag for your town or village. It would need to have the name of the town, a slogan inviting people to visit and a design showing what is special about it, e.g. a beach umbrella, a boat or a shell for a seaside town; a book or a tower for a university town etc.

Ride round the Sun. Design a poster for the first space shuttle to take passengers round the sun and into space. Again the message must be simple, but very exciting e.g.

Chinese banners. Make long Chinese banners to welcome spring, summer, autumn and winter. Decorate with Chinese-style lettering in black felt-tip pen or paint. Make and colour symbols to suggest the seasons. Make these banners very beautiful. Let them hang in the hall or, better still, on trees outside in the school grounds. They will move and sway in a light breeze. You may be able to copy some authentic Chinese greetings, as banners are often used in welcome.

Newspapers

Display of collage pictures using cut newsprint

This is one medium with which all children are familiar. The production of a class/school newspaper gives the children practice, not only in writing, but in working co-operatively. It also gives an added incentive to produce work quickly and accurately. The newspaper format looks very professional when it has been transferred to the word processor. (There are some excellent computer programs available for this kind of work.)

Discussion. Gather a selection of morning and local papers. Try to follow a current story in several different papers. Look at the variety of ways in which it is presented. Discuss the reasons.

Visits. Arrange a visit to the local newspaper office. In groups, work out a list of suitable questions before you go so that you can talk with the staff to find out who does what and how. Take notebooks and work like newspaper reporters. Write up the story of your visit and present it as a newspaper article for others to read. Take a camera loaded with black and white film and make a photographic record of your visit to go with the story. (It is best to find out if you may take photographs before you go.)

ACTIVITIES

Research. Look at your selection of newspapers. Find out about the task of the editor. Look for all the different sections in one newspaper e.g. editorial, sports desk, national/international news, local news, letters, reviews, special interest (gardens etc.), radio and TV programmes etc.

Newspapers

Class newspaper. Organise the production of your own class newspaper. Appoint an editor (or editorial board). Work out the various sections you want to include. Use the list you have compiled in your discussion. You will usually have an editorial column, sports news, local news, reviews etc. as above. Special Interests should take account of the hobbies and interests of as many children as possible – anything from pigeon racing to coin collecting is valid. Make the contributions so full of information and interest that others will want to take part too. Encourage a lively style of writing.

Decide how often the newspaper is to be published. Is it a one-off project? Once per term? Or every second Friday for one term only? Remember, it is quite an undertaking – gathering material, editing, paste-up, proof-reading, transcribing, distributing etc. Try to involve all the people in the class in the production. If you have visited the local newspaper office send a copy of your paper to the staff.

Those on your Sports section should have some knowledge of the game/sport on which they are reporting. Have a collectors' column where collectors can share their interests. Try a small ads section – parents are always delighted to find outlets for outgrown school uniform, football boots etc. Have a cookery column. Ask the staff/governors/parents to send their favourite recipe. Try a Leisure section for jokes and games. You might organise a competition for the youngest children and offer a small prize.

From long ago. Produce a special newspaper to reflect the locality as it was thirty, forty, fifty years ago. Send your reporters to residential homes (by arrangement) and talk about memories with the elderly residents. Ask parents and grandparents to provide stories and photographs of the area. Visit the local church and talk with the priest/vicar. There are usually well-kept records of times past. The local council may also be pleased to help in such a project. (Lots of opportunity for letter-writing.)

Read a story, write a story. Read a story to the class (anything from 'The Three Little Pigs' to a Roald Dahl short story). Get the children to write their version as it might appear in a newspaper. For infants, draw pencil columns on the page and ask the children to write in columns as in a newspaper. Illustrate in black and white.

Traditional story retold as news item

Further writing activities

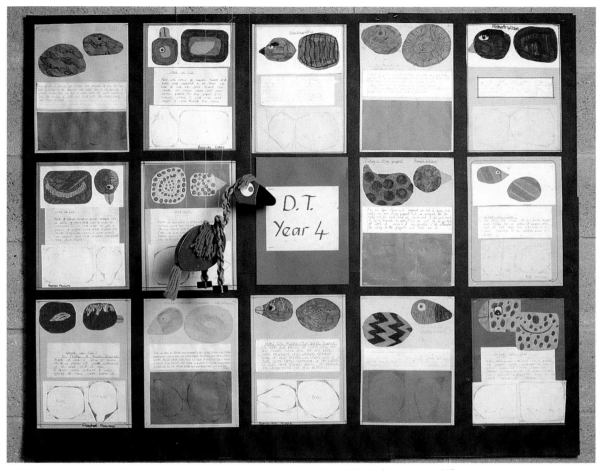

Design and technology work displayed with notes and captions (see page 47)

MESSAGES

This is a low-key form of writing, but one which is very important in everyday living. If a message is left for the milkman, for mother, for the next-door neighbour, it is important that it is accurate, succinct and gives all the information required.

Telephone messages. Offer to look after the telephone if the headteacher and secretary are unavailable. It is important that you give the name of the school and perhaps the number clearly. Ask politely if there is a message for the head, then write it down. Be sure that you have taken the number for the return call (read it back to the caller to be sure that it is correct), and any important piece of information to be passed on. Leave a note, clearly and neatly written, so that the secretary/headteacher will know who has contacted the school, the reason for the call and where they can get in touch with the caller.

Note day. Have a day/morning when everything has to be written down. No talking allowed (the teachers will love it!). All communication with teachers or friends must be in written form. Make your message short, giving only the necessary information – you are not writing a letter, simply passing on a message.

Scrambling. Make up a silly or unlikely message e.g. 'The Martians are dropping in for breakfast on Friday morning at 7.35 a.m. Please have some fried cornflakes and toasted beetles ready. They want to return by 12 noon.' Pass this in a whisper, from person to person, and see what it comes out like at the other end. The last person has to write down the message.

Further writing activities

Crack the Code. Make up a message in code. Do you remember the old favourite? YY U R, YY U B, I C U R YY 4 me! (Too wise you are, too wise you be, I see you are too wise for me!) Imagine that you are a famous detective/cunning thief/escaping prisoner and make up a message in code to tell your chief/mate/family what is happening. The only trouble is that you have forgotten to pass on the key to the code. Get your friend to try cracking your coded message. Change places.

LEAFLETS

Leaflets and brochures pass on information in quite a formal way, often using illustrations as an essential part of the package.

Collect a number of different leaflets and brochures. Discuss why they have been produced: simple information (a train timetable), getting us to change our ways (a healthy eating pamphlet), trying to sell us something (holiday brochure). Work in groups and plan how to produce leaflets in each category.

A 'healthy eating' pamphlet in lunchbox shape

School Brochure. Make up a school information leaflet. Make it suitable for parents of children new to the school. Decide what information they need e.g. school times, price of school meals, uniform details, classroom numbers (perhaps with a plan of the school), names of teaching staff etc. Then put in something about what the school is like e.g. who looks after you if you don't feel well; about assemblies, school camp, games; what you like best/least; the games you play in the playground etc. Make the school sound interesting and inviting. Illustrate your brochure.

School Camp. Make a leaflet to persuade younger children to join you on camp next time round. Tell about the meals, tents, washing facilities, visits. Explain what work you do on camp, what you do when it rains. Include photographs and illustrations. Make it sound exciting, rather like a holiday brochure.

Wacky Inventions. Design a crazy machine e.g. to weigh an elephant, to paint a high ceiling without getting covered in paint, to dust cobwebs from the stars etc. You can be as silly as you like. Make a leaflet to go with your invention with diagrams, information, price and why the rest of us should go out and buy it! Make it a very tempting offer.

How to paint a high ceiling without getting in a mess

Hobbies. Write a leaflet giving information about your hobby. Tell if there are societies you can join and give addresses. Tell how you first start, if there is any equipment you need, if there are safety rules to follow, if there are certificates you get as you become more proficient. Make your leaflet reflect your own interest and enjoyment in the hobby.

BOOK REVIEWS

This is a form of writing which makes considerable demands on primary-age children. They must condense the story, so that the flavour of the writing comes through, yet they should not give away the plot. Then they must try to give some personal judgement on what they have read. It is quite a sophisticated activity which requires a good deal of practice.

Children often tend to find book reviews boring, both to read and to write. This should be an occasional activity, not one tacked on every time a child reads a library book. Suggest reviewing three favourite books for the term: one a book of poems, one an adventure story, one a biography. Suggest review swaps, so that within a group all the books are reviewed at least once, but nobody has to review all the books he/she has read. (Mandatory book reviews can be a great disincentive to reading!)

Find the Top Ten. Organise a questionnaire to discover the Top Ten sports/horse/adventure/cookery/poetry books. Work on lively reviews which will encourage others to read the books too. Use quotes and illustrations.

Book Jacket Reviews. When you write your own book (see book section), get a friend to read it and write a 'come-on' review for the jacket i.e. one which a publisher would commission so that readers would buy the book.

Television review. Write a review of the best/worst television programme which you have watched over the last week. Give reasons why you liked/disliked it.

Further writing activities

SONG LYRICS

For children who enjoy writing in rhyme and have a good ear for rhythm, song lyrics offer a wonderful opportunity. It is a form of writing with which they are all familiar through pop songs, TV jingles, hymns – even nursery rhymes and finger plays.

Listening. Listen to a selection of tapes offering a variety of songs. Try to write down some of the words. See how much sense they make when divorced from the music. Discuss what makes a good song: words or music; or both, making a pleasing whole.

Find tapes of folk music (which usually has a strong beat) and try to write new words to old songs. Work in groups. First decide on the theme for each song, then put together some verses which can be sung to the music. You might like to use a rhyming dictionary to help.

Hymns. Use well known hymn tunes and make up-to-date words to go with them. Write hymns to be sung at Easter, Christmas, Harvest etc.

Television Jingles. Make a lively television jingle to advertise your school meals/summer camp/ jumble sale.

Green World Songs. Make up songs to encourage people to think more about our beautiful world. Find out about the Save the Seal Pup/Dolphin/Panda campaigns and make verses to suit. You can make music to fit the words using percussion instruments and shakers. Record your songs on tape.

Weather Songs. Write songs in praise of snow, sunshine, rain etc. Make your own music to accompany them. Sing the songs at assembly. Paint pictures to go with them.

Sing a song of Ten-pence. Use the old nursery rhyme 'Sing a Song of Six-pence' as a guide and make up your own up-to-date nursery song to fit the tune. Make the song very jokey – after all, what is a 'pocketful of rye'? Try adapting other nursery rhymes.

SCRIPTS

Bringing dialogue to life is difficult, but a skill which is well worth learning. Many children enjoy writing and acting in their own play, although they can get bogged down in detail.

It might be possible to have a scriptwriter visit the school, funded by an Arts Council grant. A professional will help the children to plan the action before they set about the task of script writing. He/she will discuss ideas and situations in an ordered fashion and the play will come to life over a number of weeks.

However, it is often better to begin with a familiar piece of dialogue within a well-recognised situation e.g. child/parent argument over pocket money, bedtime, doing homework. Let the children work in pairs, each taking a part. Let the dialogue develop, then ask them to write down the important phrases. Use a different coloured pen for each character. Make the piece short. Try the script out on the rest of the group. When some work has been done on simple two-character dialogue, let a group prepare a sketch taken from a folk tale (Three Billy Goats Gruff, perhaps), a Bible scene (The Good Samaritan) or from a story poem.

Alice/Pooh Bear/The Hobbit. Read a scene from a well-known story. Work as a group and try to put together a short play using the characters in the story. Give everybody something to say using the kind of language that is in the original story. You might like to change the original situation e.g. put Alice on a plane that is going to Majorca, Pooh Bear and Piglet on the London Underground, The Hobbit turning up at school.

The Owl and the Pussycat. Read Edward Lear's poem. Think about the characters that the poet might have thought of first, who *didn't* make it into the poem. Did he think about a dinosaur? a slug? a crocodile? Make up a play from the poem and give these other creatures a part.

COMIC STRIPS

'The Wrong Spell', 'The Werewolf' and 'The Runaway-bride'

This is a style of writing that much appeals to most children, especially if they enjoy drawing. To be successful at story telling through the comic strip, it is important to work through a careful planning stage. The comic strip should be planned in step-by-step episodes, with few characters and some punchy dialogue. It is an excellent way-in to use of direct speech in story writing.

QUESTIONNAIRES

Children enjoy using a questionnaire and working from a clipboard when they are researching for a project. It is a useful skill to be able to put together a set of questions which guides an interview in the right direction, so that each answer builds on the one before. Children should be encouraged to look for open questions (those that can't be answered by a simple 'yes' or 'no'). Suggest ten or twelve questions for an interview with a parent or teacher, a professional at a particular job or someone knowledgeable in an area of history, the environment, the locality. Encourage the children to note down answers in rough, then to transcribe these at a later date.

Questionnaire to Grown-ups on books they read as children.

1. Roughly what age were you when you read the book first?
2. Did you read it more than once?
3. Who was your favourite character and why?
4. Why was the book your favourite?
5. What was the best/most interesting/most exciting part of the book?
6. Was there any part of the book that was frightening, or that you did not like?
7. What category would you put it in? e.g. adventure, humour etc.
8. Was it set in the countryside, abroad, town etc?
9. Do you think that modern day children would enjoy reading it?
10. Was it set in any particular time in history?
11. Have you any other comments on the book?

(See results in display photograph on facing page.)

Make up questionnaires to find out what people think about an aspect of local government; what changes children would like to see in the playground area; the jobs people do – why they like/ dislike them; what old people remember about their childhood etc.

Before children go out on an educational visit, work out a questionnaire so that they will know what to ask of those who show them around. Use the literature about the cathedral/castle/museum to help you. Work in groups to put together a questionnaire before you visit a factory or office e.g. a newspaper office.

CROSSWORDS

It requires a fairly logical mind to make up a crossword. Use a made-up book of crosswords for children. Study how they are put together. Look at the clues. Do a few of the puzzles, then use the answers and make up new clues. Finally ask the children to make up new crosswords from scratch. Work in groups or pairs, making up and working through each other's crossword.

An interesting way of presenting factual results (see Questionnaire on facing page)

REPORTS

It is useful for children to be able to report on games, visits, their own progress in a succinct, literate way. Touches of humour should also be encouraged. Children's reports can be used in class newspapers and magazines, in assembly and on school radio. It is important to point out that a report should be as factual as possible.

Report on any new building going on near the school. Go along to a meeting (of the PTA, the parish council) and report back to the others at school. Report on new fashions, new records, new books.

NOTES

Making notes from books, papers and encyclopaedias is an under-rated skill. Any kind of research demands a high level of note-taking. Encourage children to use reference books and to make notes which can then be worked on for projects and wall displays. Use diagrams and illustrations where appropriate.

Design and technology. Practice in note-taking enables children to make explanatory captions to accompany display work in DT, science and history (see photograph on page 41).

Books

There is something satisfying about a book as an object; complete in itself, portable and full of riches for anyone who can read. The making of a book is, therefore, a very satisfying activity for children. It allows them to combine their developing literacy skills with the skills of design and the practical problems of producing a finished article. There is the excitement of creating something which can be shared and enjoyed by others. Handling the completed book brings a sense of a job well done. It establishes the child as an author.

From their first days at infant school, children can be encouraged to make, illustrate and write their own books. When young children are presented with a simple, four-paged 'book' made from sugar paper, there is the promise of a successful outcome very easily – the title page followed by three pictures and a few simple words, perhaps printed by the teacher. In a very short time they have created their own book, one which they can 'read' for themselves. There is always the comforting thought that, should they be unhappy with that particular piece of work, they can have a new start without the unsuccessful attempts being on show for a couple of months as they would be in a conventional exercise book. Make a new book for each topic so that the children have the opportunity to make a fresh start each time.

As children develop their writing and presentational skills their books should reflect this progress. Books should be of varying size and shape and should be made from a range of materials: coloured paper, wrapping paper, card, cloth, homemade paper, wallpaper. Find out different ways of binding books, different methods of making the covers. Experiment with zig-zag books, books with pockets, pop-up books. Above all, children should be encouraged to explore a variety of writing styles and attempt a range of content: from story to biography, from legend to science fiction, from straightforward information to comic strips. Books can be written by individuals, by groups or as a whole school project. They can be handwritten or typed, word-processed and printed. The making of books opens a treasure chest of opportunity. It encourages creativity, improves reading and language skills and provides children with a rare sense of achievement.

EARLY INFANT BOOKS

Make four-paged booklets to follow the seasons/festivals. Trace around a card outline and cut sugar paper into an appropriate shape e.g. leaf for autumn, apple for Harvest Thanksgiving, mask for Hallowe'en, Catherine wheel for Guy Fawkes, stable/Father Christmas sack for Christmas, snowman for winter etc. (see photograph on page 51). Tackle one page at a time. Use wax crayons for the illustrations. Talk with each child about his picture and ask an adult to write a one-line phrase to go with it. Have the child 'read' it back. The children can underwrite, overwrite or copy a single word on each page (see photographs in Beginning Writing section).

I Like/I Can/I Wish Books. Make a four-paged A5 book. Get the children to copy 'I like/I can/I wish' on each page and draw a picture. Add the words required so that each child makes his own book. Encourage him to read it back so that he becomes familiar with the 'I like' etc. phrase (see photographs in Beginning Writing section).

Zig-Zag Books. Either take a familiar story or create a new one with the children suggesting characters and situations. Use a clip-board to note down ideas and assemble the finished illustrated story in zig-zag form. Stand it up on a display table. Encourage the children to read the story to one another.

Alphabet Books. Use the zig-zag or concertina form and make a book with pictures beginning with the sounds of the letters in the alphabet. Make sure that the sound is phonetically correct e.g. sun, sea, salt for 's', not sugar; witch, water, windmill for 'w', not whale; tree, tank, tomahawk for 't', not thimble.

Wall story based on Maurice Sendak's book *Where the Wild Things Are* **(published by The Bodley Head)**

Wall Story. Read a familiar story, *Cinderella, Three Little Pigs, Three Bears* etc. and have the children illustrate each episode. Write the synopsis underneath each picture and put it on the wall where it is easy for the children to read (see photograph above).

What's the Time? Use a clock stamp on every page of a book made from A4 paper. Write 'At 7 o'clock I get up. At 8 o'clock I have breakfast. At 9 o'clock I go to school.' etc. throughout the day. Match the time on the clock stamp to the sentence. This book can also be made zig-zag fashion as a class/group book.

Weather Books. Make shaped weather books, umbrella for rain, sun for sunshine, leaf for wind etc. Collect a mini-thesaurus of rain/wind/sun words and zap them across the pages in appropriate colours using bright felt-tips. Make a design of the words e.g. dazzling/shining/ fiery/burning for sunshine.

A mini-thesaurus of weather words

When I Grow Up. Make a class book with individual paintings and a written sentence e.g. Alice wants to be a policewoman, Mark wants to be an actor, Sarah wants to be Prime Minister etc. Use lots of repetition.

Journey to the Moon. Make books shaped like space-craft. Talk about the preparations the children would make. Talk about the food/clothes/books they would need. Discuss what they might see on the moon, how they are going to get there and back, the first thing they would want to do on landing back home. Take a page for each idea. Start each page with a sentence e.g. 'I will need . . .' and follow with a list: goggles, hot-water bottle, moon map, 25 tubes of Smarties, a photograph of my mum etc. Draw pictures of all the items.

Early infant season books (see page 48)

Christmas Books. Make stable-shaped books which open to tell the Christmas story. For top infants or lower juniors the child could choose to tell the story from the point of view of one of the characters e.g. Ben, the boy shepherd; Dorcas, the innkeeper's daughter; Hassan, the King's camelkeeper etc.

House Books. Make a book in a simple house shape. Title it 'My House'. Inside make each page a separate room in the house: 'This is the kitchen.' Draw and name all the things found in the kitchen. This type of work makes an ideal introduction to 'key' phonics.

PROGRESSION

As children become more confident and capable, the standards expected of their writing should rise accordingly. It may be that within one class of top infants, there will be some children writing at junior level, using complete sentences, interesting images and a range of connectors. At the same time others may still be at the one word stage. Writing is a very individual skill and the teacher should judge each child's work at his/her own level. Often one can use the same starter idea, but demand different outcomes according to individual capability.

As they become more expert both in writing and in assembling books, the children should be encouraged to experiment with different ways of making them. Have a range of materials available: different colours and textures of papers, a choice of mark-makers, glue, binding tape, staples, needle and cotton etc. Make a collection of books which show new ideas: miniature books, pop-ups, pocketed books, flap books, zig-zags. Discuss with the children how they could adapt these ideas for themselves.

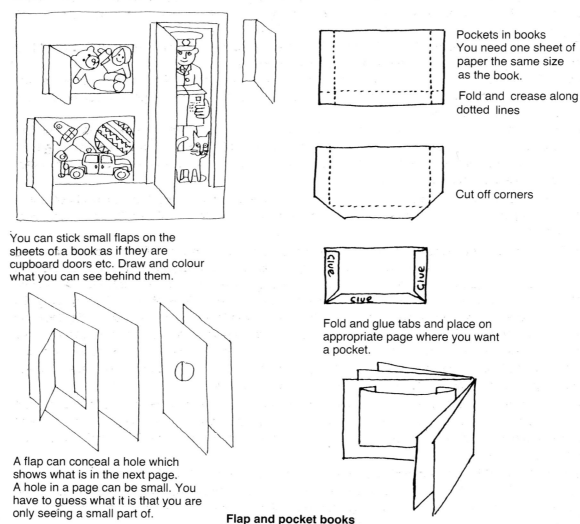

You can stick small flaps on the sheets of a book as if they are cupboard doors etc. Draw and colour what you can see behind them.

A flap can conceal a hole which shows what is in the next page. A hole in a page can be small. You have to guess what it is that you are only seeing a small part of.

Pockets in books
You need one sheet of paper the same size as the book.

Fold and crease along dotted lines

Cut off corners

Fold and glue tabs and place on appropriate page where you want a pocket.

Flap and pocket books

BOOK COVERS

Encourage children to see the cover of their book as part of an integral design. Try out marbling, collage, felt, card, woven paper etc. Book-making is an art form in its own right.
(For instruction on marbling technique, please turn to page 72.)

Story writing

Books are so versatile that they can provide us with fantasy, humour, adventure, information and more. We should give children the opportunity to try out as many of these different strands of literature as possible, both in reading and in writing. Story-writing in all its forms, however, is the content most often associated with book-making in the classroom. It is one of the most difficult writing tasks to set young children, although a successful story book brings enormous pleasure to the writer – and indeed to the reader. It is exciting to be able to take the reader off to another land, another time, perhaps, and to build pictures in his/her imagination.

To help children from early juniors onwards to tackle story-writing with success, we provide a guide which takes the writer from the first idea through to publication.

STEPS IN STORY-WRITING

1. **Story-planning**. Children should be encouraged to develop the habit of planning their stories before they begin to write. They should use it as a guide, not as an immutable structure – stories can take off in unexpected directions as one writes! Use an A4 sheet doubled to give four A5 pages, big enough for notes, too small for the story in its finished form.

Page 1. Ask the question, 'Who is the story for?' (i.e. audience – is it for infants, my friends, Mum and Dad?) Decide on a working title and the main characters.

Page 2. Synopsis of the story. This technique gives practice in the skills of note-making. Sometimes children are tempted to try and write the whole story at this stage. Encourage them to keep it to a skeletal outline.

Page 3. Think about how you want the story to end. This helps the writer to look ahead, to do his/her problem-solving in advance. It also encourages slow writers to know that an end is in sight!

Page 4. Leave blank for notes and questions which may arise from the editorial conference, or for deviations as the story progresses.

2. **First Draft**. The children should rough out the story, not worrying too much about either handwriting or spelling. The golden rule is that they must be able to read the draft. Use scrap paper for this stage.

3. **Editorial Conference**. Try to encourage the children to form an 'editorial board' (with the teacher as facilitator until they get into the swing of things). Working from the first draft, ask one child to give the general outline of his story, and then choose a page or a chapter to read aloud. The others should think about what they have heard and ask questions of the writer e.g. 'Why did the bank robber need the money?', 'How did the children get to the moon?' or better still, 'How did they get home again?' Encourage the children to look for weaknesses and inconsistencies. They may find this difficult at first, but their skills will improve as time goes on. It is important that the group learns to offer positive criticism – and children can be very generous in this respect. Story-planning tends to become much tighter after working in this kind of way.

4. **Re-drafting**. When the writer is satisfied with both the plan and the first draft and has thought about the questions raised by the editorial board, she should then discuss details of grammar and spelling with the teacher. This stage should be on a one-to-one basis, if possible. This is where the teaching is done.

5. **Final Draft**. This is the easy bit, all downhill from now on. Each child should feel responsible for making his final draft as good as possible: correct spelling and punctuation – and it should be legible. This may indeed be the final stage for some of the books i.e. they are ready to go 'public'. If this is the case, the children will want to illustrate their books.

6. **Typed-up/word-processed script**. Some of the books can be put on the word processor or be typed up. This makes a professional job of the children's work and at least one book by each child should be done in this way every session. The manuscript should be proof-read by the author.

Story writing

7. **Art-work**. Illustrations for the typed/word-processed books should be in black pen, so that they can be easily photocopied. If necessary, they can be coloured later.

8. **'Cut and Paste' Stage**. The scripts should be cut and assembled with the illustrations, then pasted in position, ready for photocopying. Take care with the page numbering where pages are to be folded.

9. **Cover**. The children should spend some time on the cover, recognising it as an integral part of the overall book design. Either print the title with care or use stencils or 'Letraset'.

10. **Final Assembly**. Make multiple copies of each book to be published (6–10 is a reasonable number). After photocopying, the books may be stapled or sewn. The children may wish to colour both cover and illustrations for a few of their books, so that they have some full-colour ones to give away, place in the school library, sell etc.

11. **Reading and Sharing**. The author should be given the opportunity to share in the achievement of the published book. She should be encouraged to read the story aloud, or have the teacher read it, to its planned audience. Sharing one's story is part of the joy of writing.

12. **Congratulations**. The author should be presented with six copies of his book. Try to make sure that he has pleasure in reading and handling the published book. Only then will he become conscious of the excitement and power of writing.

The Witch on the Mountain
By Dean Benden

Once upon a time a witch lived in a castle on a mountain. She was a happy witch. She had glasses on, and a big pointed hat. One day she tried a spell, but it didn't work. Then she turned round and saw a very big spider behind her. She ran around the room and the big spider got dizzy and the spider fell down and the witch had a big smile on her face.

The next day God said to the witch, "A big snake is coming today," and the big snake came. The witch said, "Can I measure you, Snake?" So she did and she tied the snake up. Then God gave her a box of gold and she was rich.

Then she went to the wood where it was dark, and it was spooky in the wood. Then an ugly man caught her and she was pushed into a dark dungeon.

- 2 -

Then the witch saw a man with a beard. His feet were dirty and he was an old man. He was trapped in the dungeon too. The witch thought hard, and she made a magic spell. Suddenly they saw a flying carpet and the witch and the old man got on the carpet. They flew through the air and escaped from the dungeon. They landed back at the witch's castle on the mountain.

Book making

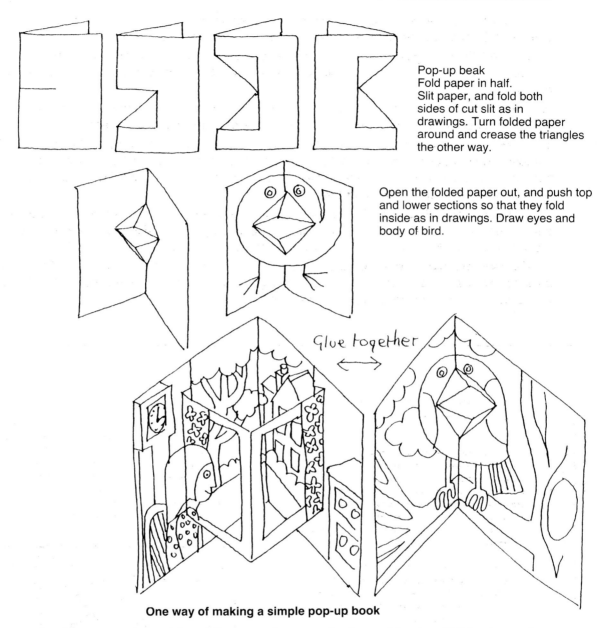

Pop-up beak
Fold paper in half.
Slit paper, and fold both
sides of cut slit as in
drawings. Turn folded paper
around and crease the triangles
the other way.

Open the folded paper out, and push top
and lower sections so that they fold
inside as in drawings. Draw eyes and
body of bird.

Glue together

One way of making a simple pop-up book

Most good writing stems from rich reading experience and a love of books. Children's reading should be as varied as possible so that their writing will reflect this variety of style and richness of content. It goes without saying that a range of books should be easily accessible to children at every stage of the school. They should be encouraged to use class and school libraries and to explore the treasure house of the public library. They must be encouraged to borrow books to read at home and it is important to set aside time for silent reading in the classroom so that children establish the habit of reading. The teacher should also be seen to read at her own level at some time during the day.

Visits. Visit the public library. Ask the librarian to explain the system of cataloguing, of book-borrowing, using the computer, and generally de-mystifying the business of visiting the library. Work in groups: ask the children to find out what is available on local history, get them to find three or four books on their own particular hobby or interest, use the children's section to find books by favourite authors, look for biographies which add information to the current history topic etc. Find out what else happens in the library, e.g. art displays, information on local events, tapes and CDs, story-reading sessions.

Discussion. Talk about what kind of book children enjoy reading. Make a list of different types of story: adventure, biography, fantasy, mystery, ghost stories, animal stories, true stories, war stories, science fiction, fairy stories and legends, history, information and DIY books, comics etc.

ACTIVITIES

Make a display of books on local history. Use old photographs and artefacts. Ask elderly people to talk about the town/village as it was. Look for old recipes, newspapers, postcards, family Bibles etc.

Make a display of books enjoyed by teachers, parents and Governors as children. Ask them to write on a postcard why they liked them so much. Use old school photographs and scenes from their family albums (see display photograph on page 47).

ADVENTURE

Treasure Island. Work in groups to produce a Treasure Island map. Either individually or in twos, children can work out adventures which take place on the island. Imagine being shipwrecked, following clues to the treasure, finding enough food to eat on the island, making a boat, rigging up signals to get back home. Think of the heat, the hunger, the loneliness, the lack of books, TV etc. Tell about how you miss home, make friends with the islanders, find your way home – with or without the treasure.

Magic Carpet. Take an adventure on a magic carpet to unknown lands. Use holiday brochures to exotic places to give you ideas. Would the ride be as smooth as an aeroplane? Would you need passports? Would the carpet fly to a timetable? Who would go with you? Where would you land? Discuss ideas in a group before you start.

Journey to Outer Space. Gather information about space by looking at books and encyclopaedias. Work out your route and destination. How long would the journey take? What would the planets look like? How would you survive? Imagine a race through space, being chased by space monsters in their GTi spacemobiles. You are boarded by these three-eyed, four-eared lime green creatures. They threaten to zap you with lasers. What happens next? How do you outwit them? How do you get back home?

Gulliver Land. Imagine getting a shiny magic penny (given by Grandpa, Aunt Nellie, old Mr. McPherson for your birthday). You wonder what on earth you can buy with a penny – not much, you think. You rub it in your hands and Kerwhoosh! you are as big as a giant/as small as an ant. What happens next?

The Great Detective. The people next door have lost a jewel/the keys to the safe/their baby. You, the Great Detective, find a clue which the police have overlooked. Tell about following the clues to where the robber is to be found. Tell how you outwit the robber and bring the jewel/keys/baby back to your delighted nextdoor neighbour. You might be interviewed by the papers, the radio, television.

Adventure Serial. Work as a group. Together read the first chapter of an adventure story. Draw lots to decide who goes next. That person writes chapter 2, and so on. You might all get together to think about the ending.

Book making

BIOGRAPHY

Granny's Baby. Talk to your grandparents or older relatives. Ask about Mum/Dad as a baby and a small child. Ask what they looked like, what they liked to eat, what they did when they didn't like the food!, if they had a pet name, what naughty things they did. Take a notebook and make notes from your talk. Then write out the story of your parents' childhood as if you were beginning their biography.

Favourite Character from history. Choose a famous character from your history topic. Find out as much as you can about the person. Make notes from library books and encyclopaedias. Write out the story of their life. If you can find diaries they have written you might be able to write the story as an autobiography, pretending you are that person.

Unknowns. Choose another person from history, but this time make it someone we haven't heard about. Make it a slave, maid, clerk, jester etc. who worked for a famous historic person. Think about Queen Elizabeth I's lady-in-waiting, King Arthur's court jester, a sailor on Captain Bligh's 'Bounty', a soldier in one of the great battles. Find out as much as you can about the life and times of the famous person, then write the biography of someone unknown who was watching and listening to what was going on at the time.

Portraits. Find a photograph in a newspaper or in a library book, or bring one from home that interests you. Think about the person in the photograph. Make up a name, a family, a job etc. for the person. Use your imagination to work out where he/she was born, what his/her mother and father were like, (or imagine that the person was found on a doorstep as a baby and brought up in a Home). Invent a life-story and write a biography from it. Illustrate your book with 'photographs' taken as a baby, a child, a young person and grown-up. Give dates etc. as in a real biography.

Herbert Bear. Use your favourite toy, one which you had as a baby. Make up a life story for him, how he was made, where he was bought, when he was given to you, adventures he has had in your company – like this, perhaps: 'Herbert Bear was born in a noisy factory in Oldham. He was brown and furry and very cuddly. Aunt Jenny saw him on the shelf of a shop in Bath. She fell in love with him. Aunt Jenny was too grown-up to have a bear of her own, so she gave Herbert to a little boy called David.' What happened next?

INFORMATION

Hobbies and Interests. Write about your own hobby or interest – stamp-collecting, pigeon-racing, football, orienteering, coin-collecting etc. Make your book informative and exciting. Give details of where you can join a club or get magazines with all the up-to-date news of your hobby. Tell others what you do, describe the people you meet, tell about the day things went wrong and what keeps you going. Give information to those who would like to take up your hobby. You might like to present a talk and show your book at assembly. You may be surprised how many other children would like to know more!

A playground game. Describe your favourite playground game in such a way that someone who has never played would know the rules. You might like to include a diagram if it is a team game, so that people know where they should stand if they are defence or attack. It is a good idea to exchange games with a school in another part of the country as part of a pen-friend scheme. You will be surprised to find that many of the games are similar to yours, but have a different name or use different counting rhymes etc.

Things to do while ill in bed. Work as a class or group. Gather all the good ideas you have for things that keep you occupied when you are ill in bed. They must not be too messy! Try to remember what kept you quiet when you had mumps or chickenpox. Take a page or two each and give instructions, with pictures of your best idea. (Perhaps it is making paper dolls, finger puppets, a card game for one, making masks from paper plates, reading a favourite book and working out a new ending.) This book would be a best-seller among the mums and dads.

Paper boxes
Make a box out of one piece of paper

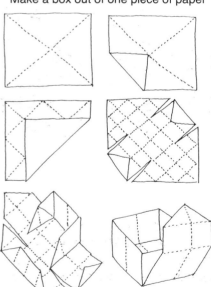

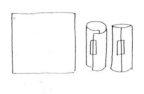

Finger puppets
You need pieces of paper a little longer than your finger and wide enough to wrap around it and fasten with adhesive tape. Press the paper flat and decorate, using scissors, felt-tip pens and glue etc.

Simple weaving
Cut parallel lines ½″ from the end of a piece of paper. Cut strips of coloured magazine paper and weave into slotted paper.

A rocking animal
Fold a piece of paper in half. Cut 2 slits and a curve on the open edges. Cut suitable shapes for head and tail. Fold and bend and slot into place as in drawings.

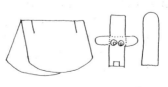

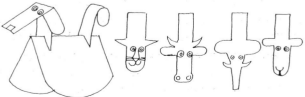

Making a Garden. Collect ideas for making gardens in the classroom or indoors at home. Tell about growing beans in a jar, making a mini-garden in a foil plate, growing carrot tops, growing plants from pips etc. Make this a very colourful book with lots of do-it-yourself diagrams that others can follow.

How to make a mini garden

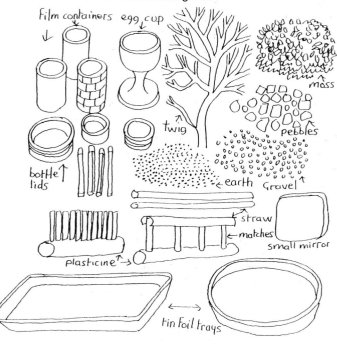

You will need small containers to keep flowers fresh. These can be painted or covered with paper painted to look like stone or brick. All the ingredients for your garden need to be small to keep the mini scale. Other objects can be made out of cardboard.

Christmas Gifts. Make a book of ideas for making Christmas gifts and cards. These should be things that don't need a lot of expensive materials. You will find some of these ideas in books and on television programmes like 'Blue Peter'. Try them out for yourself and then write down a list of the things that you need (thin card, scissors, felt-tip pens, glue), how to go about it, then draw a picture of the finished article or card. This would make a good book to sell at the Christmas Fair. (You could ask each of the teachers to contribute an idea too.)

How to . . . Books. Make a book to show how to take care of your pet/look after your teeth/groom your pony etc. This should be on a topic you know well – no use writing about grooming a pony if you haven't had a go yourself. Make a list of the things you need, how you should go about things, what you need to know about pets/teeth/ponies etc. Make it easy for others to follow.

Mini-thesaurus. Make a mini-thesaurus to go with your topic work. Look for words you might like to use, 'colour' words, 'magic' words, 'time' words etc. and put them together with pictures and a note about the meaning of the word. Put words with similar meanings together so that your use of English is wide and varied. You can also make classroom dictionaries in the same way.

Book making

BOOKS WRITTEN FOR YOUNGER CHILDREN

When you write for four, five and six-year-olds you must write in a special way. The sentences should not be too long. You can use a lot of repetition i.e. use the same words and phrases over and over again. Don't be too worried about using long words now and again. Young children like the sound of words like 'elephant' and 'rhinoceros', 'dinosaur' and 'pterodactyl' – and, of course, you can make pictures of those words because they are all nouns. Keep your stories short. Use lots of pictures. Try making flap books.

Flap Books. Little children enjoy using flap books. Make a book for them which has animals or toys hidden behind flaps. Ask questions in the story. Kate has lost her teddy bear. Where is he hiding? Is he in the cupboard? No, there's a sweeping brush in the cupboard. Is he under the bed? No, there's a pair of slippers under the bed. And so on. Put in lots of repetition and make your drawings very colourful (see photograph on facing page).

What's in Grandad's pocket? Use a modified zig-zag format to make a flap book with pockets. On each page print the question 'What's in Grandad's/Aunt Emily's/mother kangaroo's pocket?' Young children will enjoy opening the pockets to find out what is hidden inside. The repetition in the captions will help their reading. You can use the same idea for 'Who lives in this house?' showing a dog in its kennel, pig in its sty etc. Try also 'Who is hiding behind the chair/under the bed/in the kitchen cupboard?' (see photograph opposite).

The Very Hungry Ladybird. Think about what a ladybird likes to eat and start with 'On Sunday the Very Hungry Ladybird ate one . . .' and so on, getting more and more outrageous, until at last it eats seven Knickerbocker Glories, or something like that. Cut holes in the pages so that you can see where the ladybird has been eating. You should be able to see pictures of her food through the holes.

Mini-books. Make very little books with only a word or two (very neatly printed) on each page. Make tiny pictures to go with the words. You might like to write mini-books about mini-beasts like caterpillars or beetles or snails. Think about little magic creatures like goblins or leprechauns or elves or gremlins. Make tiny books for tiny creatures. Put them together in a little box.

Make a series of mini-books. Make a box the right size to keep them in.

Book making

Flap books (see facing page)

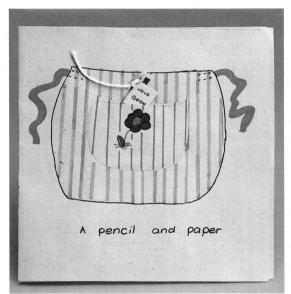

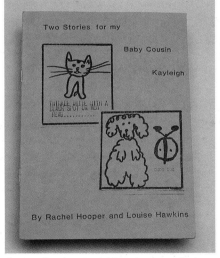

A word-processed book, one of six copies presented to the author (see page 54)

Rag Books. You might like to try rag books for very little children. Use a collage style for this. Try a book of toys, houses, things for the beach etc. Put one picture on each page and the word printed clearly in felt-tip pen or sewn in a bright colour. For the beach book you could have words like sand castle, beach ball, boat, fishing net etc., just one idea to a page. Sew the spine of your book with strong stitches so that it will take a lot of wear.

ABC Books. Make ABC books for young infants. Draw a picture on each page in alphabet order . . . one clear picture and a single word on each page. (Make sure that the word begins with the correct sound e.g. sun, snake etc. for 's', not shoe which begins with 'sh'.)

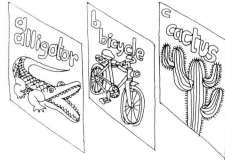

Book making

The Lost Kitten. Write a simple story about a kitten who is lost and found. Tell what happens to him when he is on his own. Is he lost in a neighbour's shed? Locked in a garage? Did he jump into a furniture van? Climb a tree? Or did something much more magic than this happen to him? Perhaps he hitched a lift on a passing snow-goose, went off with a friendly witch, climbed aboard a Starship and had to have his own special spacesuit made. Tell your story in two or three episodes and give it a happy ending. Draw lots of pictures for your young audience.

Nursery Rhymes. Have a look at a book of nursery rhymes. Use the characters to tell stories in an up-to-date way. Tell the story of Mary bringing the lamb into your school. What would the Head say? What would your teacher do? Where would Mary put her lamb while you were all at PE or in assembly? Make the stories quite funny. Remember to put in lots of pictures.

Ginger Top and the Three Hippos. Write your own version of a favourite fairy story. Change the names and alter what happens in the story. Instead of Goldilocks, try Ginger Top; instead of three bears have three hippos or four giraffes. Make your story similar to the well-known one, but not the same. Give it your individual touch. Use the same idea for your version of *The Three Little Pigs*, *Cinderella*, *The Little Red Hen* etc.

GHOST STORIES

Skeletons in the Cellar. Think of a skeleton family living in your cellar; Father Bones, Mother Bones and Baby Bones – you might even have Boney the pup and Bonikins the kitten! These skeletons are not very clever at haunting and make lots of mistakes. They try to show Baby Bones what to do, but usually get it wrong. Think of ghosts that say 'Boo!' and frighten one another. Think of ghosts that don't like the dark. Think of ghosts that get air-sick when they are flying. Make your story very funny.

Noises in the Night. Write a ghost story about something half-heard in the night. You think of all kinds of spooky things, then it turns out to have a perfectly ordinary explanation – trains shunting, owls in the treetops, a plane droning across the sky. Have a twist at the end and keep your readers guessing until the very last paragraph. Use 'bubble' pictures for this one showing a child in bed with thought bubbles for everything he/she imagines.

Noises in the night

62

Book making

I Once Lived Here. Set your story in a very old house. Make it all quite ordinary until someone feels a presence in one of the rooms. Nobody actually sees a ghost at first. Then you think you hear a voice saying 'I once lived here.' What happens next?

The Skeleton on the Train. Imagine going on a holiday in the train/going to town on the bus. Someone comes to sit beside you. A voice asks if this is the right train for London/Bristol. It is a perfectly ordinary voice, but when you turn to answer you find that it belongs to a skeleton. The skeleton does not appear to know that there is anything unusual about him. Tell what happens next. Make this a funny story, not frightening.

FANTASY

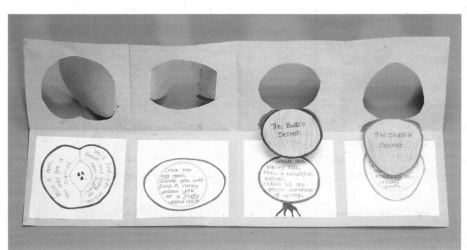

Stages in making a zig-zag flap book

Secret Worlds. Think of an apple, an egg, an orange, a fossil, a lump of coal, a conker. Think of the secrets they contain. Until you cut open the apple, crack the egg, break the fossil, nobody in the world has ever seen inside. It's a secret! Write about the new life hidden inside a conker, an orange, an egg. Write about fire hidden in the heart of coal, the colours of spring in a daffodil bulb. Begin your writing with the words 'My eyes are the first to see . . .' or 'Hidden inside is a secret . . .' Make a 'Secret Worlds' book using a modified zig-zag format. Cut flaps in the shape of the apple, orange, egg etc. and open up to reveal the hidden piece of writing (see photograph above).

Book making

Dear Mr. Wizard. Imagine that you have won a place on a 'Fix-it' programme to visit a wizard at work. Begin your story with a letter asking if you can come and stay. Think of all the things that you can learn – recipes for spells, how to fly, how to become invisible. Make the story start from what happens when you get to Merlin's cave. Is it funny or frightening? How can you help Merlin, the wizard? How do you get back home?

Letter to a wizard

Dear Mr. Merlin,

Could you fix it for me
to be a wizard for the day?
Please send an invitation –
I'd love to come and stay.

I'll get all the proper gear,
black cloak and pointed hat,
sprinkle them with star-shapes
and bring my own pet bat.

If I can be your assistant
I'll work hard all day long.
I'll stir the simmering cauldron
till spells are hot and strong.

I'll gladly add in eyes of
newts and spiders by the load
if you can fix a recipe to
turn my brother into a toad.

You're a modern man, Mr. Merlin,
I know you couldn't care less
that I'm not some ambitious boy
but an apprentice *wizardess*.

Love from
Lucy XXX

Moira Andrew

Calling Outer Space. Begin your story with the discovery of a mystery circle in the school grounds/football pitch/park. You decide, with a friend, to turn detective and find out what has made the circle in the grass. It is night. A UFO appears, lands, Outer-Spatial Beings step out. Describe what they look like, what they say, the questions they ask. Perhaps they invite you and your friend to go for a ride around the galaxy. Tell what happens. What do you tell your parents when you get home? Do they believe your story? Design a space-ship cover for your book and cut it to shape.

Through the Gate. Make a list of places, real or imaginary, which you would like to visit. Think about the colours, the sounds, the smells, the trees and flowers and buildings in these places. Build up several scenarios in note form. Think of the gate in *The Secret Garden* (by Frances Hodgson Burnett). Imagine a high wall, a gate, a silver key. Turn the key in the lock, slowly, slowly. Think how you would feel. Describe some of the wonderful scenes on the other side – because you have found a magic gateway! Use your notes to take your readers on a journey 'Through the Gate'.

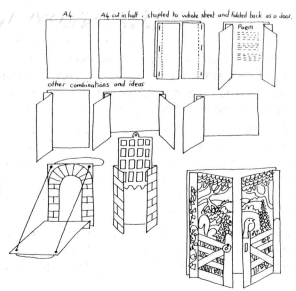

Book making

Little Monster Book. Invent a monster. Give it a long name, like Christopher's 'Butterfly-eating Miggie-Maggie Monster' or Vaughan's 'Kangaroo-killing fire-breathing Monster'. Write a story about your own monster, first describing how it looks, where it lives, what it likes to eat etc. (Be your own David Attenborough!) Make this look like a fantasy book. Make it from unusual materials; wrapping paper, wall paper, greaseproof paper. Make it with pockets and store very small books inside the pockets, each with its own separate story about the monster.

Books made from brown paper and greaseproof paper. Note the mini-book concealed in its own pocket

Starters for stories

Stories, like poems, do not fall off the shelf ready-made. It can be very difficult for children to find a way into a story and develop their idea to a rounded-off ending which satisfies both writer and reader. Teachers can often get round this problem by providing an imaginative selection of 'starters' and plenty of time to talk through the children's ideas.

Outlines. Offer outlines, rather like those on the preceding pages. Set a scene, ask open-ended questions about how they might feel in the situation, what they would see and hear, what might happen next. These discussions can take place in a group as children often spark off ideas among themselves as they talk. Encourage them to make notes of feeling words, of colour and sight and sound words. Ask the children to think how they would get back home from an adventure or some magic faraway place.

Legends and Fairy Stories. Encourage children to re-tell from existing stories, emphasising that their own story might have a new twist e.g. they might grow wings and fly alongside Icarus; they might dive beneath the ocean to swim into Neptune's palace.

'How the Whale Became'. Use Ted Hughes' delightful stories as the basis for children's own ideas on 'How the Anteater/Slug/Ladybird/Giraffe Became'. This work also encourages children to find out and make notes on animal behaviour before they work on the imaginative content.

By-standers. Use the idea of the child being in the crowd on an historic occasion. Get them to re-tell a story from history or a Biblical story from the point of view of a contemporary by-stander.

Headlines. Cut out headlines from a newspaper. Choose them carefully so that they offer open-ended possibilities e.g. 'Forgotten Island', 'The Green Wave', 'The Twilight Zone'. Use the headlines as titles for stories of adventure or mystery.

Artefacts. Gather the children into a group and produce an interesting artefact. Look at it carefully. Pass it round. Suggest where it has come from, what its history might be. Use a gold ring with a missing stone, a pocket watch with an inscription, a well-used toy or a baby's bonnet or an old recipe book – anything for which a history can be invented.

Treasure Box. Place a number of unrelated items in a box e.g. a white cup, a photograph, a pair of scissors, a withered leaf, a key, a golf ball. Ask the children to write stories (perhaps in twos) around these various things. They must try to work in as many of them as possible.

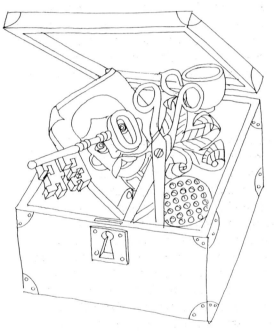

Magic Mirror. Use a set of small hand mirrors. Get the children to work in pairs. Go outside or find a dusty corner of the hall or stairway. Use the mirror to reflect something quite ordinary and everyday from an unusual angle. Build a story around this new discovery. Ask the children to superimpose their own part-reflections on the panelling/tree bark/fence post and set a story inside the mirror.

THE TEACHER'S TASK

It is important to offer suggestions, leave unanswered questions hanging in the air, to use music, painting, smells (cinnamon, lemon juice, pot pourri) to stimulate imaginative story-writing. Ask the open-ended question or suggest the next possibility to help a child along. Help him, too, to work out where a story can end. Endings can be very difficult – one needs to get away from the old 'then we had tea and went to bed. THE END' which is all too common when children are struggling with a way out of their stories.

Writing and book-making should be integrated activities as far as possible. The words and pictures should complement one another and the shape, dimension and texture of the finished book should come together to produce a total aesthetic experience for author and reader.

Beginning poetry

Listening. Listening is becoming a forgotten skill. It is, therefore, important that we teach children to listen creatively to poems and stories. Creative listening implies that listeners take an active part and that words do not simply wash over them.

Teachers can help children towards this goal by providing several short listening sessions each day. Suggest that they make pictures in the mind, but emphasise that you expect quiet courteous listening. Listen to music, nursery rhymes and stories. Young children have a well developed sense of rhyme and rhythm and traditional nursery rhymes provide an excellent introduction to listening to poetry.

When they become familiar with a number of the traditional ones, encourage the children to look for new rhymes and make up their own versions, keeping to the original pattern. Try 'Sing a song of tenpence/A barrowful of hay . . .' or 'Little Miss Fashion/Sat on a cushion/Eating her bangers and mash . . .'

Build on this kind of play with language by introducing a range of poems and rhymes from anthologies and collections. Read rhyming and non-rhyming poems. Read poems for maths, for topic work, for language and for the simple joy of words. Read favourite poems again and again, so that the children begin to store rhythm and pattern, image and story in their heads. This not only encourages active listening, but deepens and enriches their knowledge of language.

Teacher as secretary. Even before the children can write for themselves (see Beginning Writing), they are capable of using image and poetic language. One way of exploring language with young children is to appeal to their imagination. Let them look at a small beaded purse or decorated pillbox; anything that could suggest something magic hiding inside. Ask what could be in the purse, especially if it were magic. Make a list of the children's ideas, using the *middle* of the blackboard, overhead projector or clipboard. Add descriptive words to the left of the list, movement words to the right. 'Top and tail' your list and you have an instant poem. By constructing your list in three parts, you can help the children to explore a variety of language without rewriting.

The finished version of an infant group poem

When the poem has been drafted satisfactorily in list form, transfer to the wall 'in best' as in illustration.

Poetry starters

The biggest block for any writer is coming face to face with a sheet of white paper waiting for words. This is as true of children writing as it is of adults. Children want to please, but they don't know where or how to start. It is important, therefore, to provide them with a method of working and a range of ways into poetry.

Group poetry, possibly based on a clear pattern, will give confidence to those children who are uncertain. They see a poem growing from simple beginnings and come to realise that everyone's ideas count, that, unlike maths, there is no wrong answer. Suggest that the children make a 'shopping list' and 'go shopping for a poem'. This takes much of the mystique out of poetry writing. Work from 'shopping list' to 'rough' to 'best', and encourage the children to edit and redraft their writing. Follow this principle with the group poem and let the children see the process of finding the most successful words to put over what they want to say. When the children are working on an individual piece of writing and have a problem in knowing how to start transferring words and ideas from the list to rough work, the teacher can take the opportunity to help. Encourage the choice of the most unusual, personal or evocative idea as the opening line.

I find it more useful to use paper than a drafting book. When the list is on paper, the problem of turning back the page does not arise. When the poem is presented in 'best' on paper, either hand-written or word-processed and decorated, it is ready for wall display. Records of writing progress can be kept by providing a folder for each child, making sure that each piece of work is dated. It is also useful to keep the list and rough work for one or two of the pieces so that there is some record of the way in which the poem was approached. It shows too where spelling errors have occurred and what help is required.

A rule of thumb for listing and rough work is that both the child and the teacher should be able to read it. The final presentation should be as good in every respect as that particular child can make it. As a practising poet I know that there are many times when inspiration fails and one is pleased to be given a topic or a structure to work to – children often respond in the same way, so a few specific starter ideas follow. However, there are some general observations on getting started:

1. When introducing a new poetry structure, try a group poem first. This shows the kind of thing you are aiming for, and is a good confidence builder.
2. Don't expect all children to be enthused by every starter. Some will suit some individuals better than others.
3. If a competent writer suggests that he/she has a better idea or a poem simply burning to be written, let them go ahead.
4. From time to time the teacher should write alongside the children and perhaps be ready to share her work. 'Teacher as writer' has a tonic effect on the children's work.

Group poems. When working on a group poem let the children watch the process of poem-building from shopping list through rough work (making corrections as you go along) to best, or presentation stage. Encourage the children to join in and bounce words and ideas around. In this way, much lively and original language surfaces and those who have difficulty in putting words on paper are at no disadvantage.

What is the sun? Use this starter as a group or individual poem. It develops the idea of image. Ask the question 'If the sun weren't the sun, what do you think it might be?' The first imaginative leap might prove difficult, but once the children realise that they are looking for something round and yellow the ideas begin to flow. A first list might look something like this: ball, yo-yo, orange, pound coin, pancake, wheel, buttercup, dandelion. As they become bolder, the children will suggest ideas like: straw hat, lemon ice, wedding ring, pot of honey, bowl of custard. Encourage the children to extend the image so that the straw hat is 'pegged on the sky', the lemon ice is 'melting from the clouds,' the ball is 'kicked up to heaven' and so on. The trick is to keep the two ideas (the sun and its image) going along together. Suggest a fairly tight structure e.g.

What is the sun?

The sun is a lemon lolly
melting from the sky.
It is a golden pancake
tossed up to heaven.

The sun is a yellow yo-yo
bouncing on its string.
It is a hula-hoop
bowling across the universe.

The sun is a wheel
rolling into space.
It is a pound coin
dropped down the drain.

The sun is a buttercup
blowing in the breeze.
It is an orange marigold
growing in God's garden.

Follow such a group poem by individual work on a similar theme. What is the moon/rain/a star/the wind/snow?

One way of displaying 'What is the sun?' poems

Poetry starters

Looking closely. Take an easily identifiable natural object (shell, lemon, pine cone) and disguise it by wrapping it in a handkerchief. Get the children to talk about the shape and feel of the object through the wrapper – not about the object itself. Find shape and touch words. Then reveal the object and add sight, colour and hearing words. Extend some of them into similes e.g. as prickly as a hedgehog, as white as a unicorn, sounds like the sea. Combine the observational skills of the scientist with the creative skills of the poet to make a short descriptive piece. You might suggest that the children use a five line pattern. This encourages economy of language.

Modelling. Modelling allows children to try patterns and forms which other poets have used. To introduce modelling, find poems with a distinctive structure or an interesting idea which children can copy. Look for repetition (in chorus form, perhaps), pattern or zaniness. With infants it may be enough to replace a single word or phrase, while for older children the starter may provide a springboard to something wholly new.

List poems. You can develop your shopping list into a poem. Put together a list of your favourite/ least favourite foods, things you find in the attic, in your pocket, presents in Father Christmas's sack, things you pack in the suitcase for going on holiday. Perhaps allow only two words in each line e.g. 'Sticky sweets/Rubber bands/Chewed gobstoppers/Horrible hands!' If your poem is meant to be funny, you might try and make the list poem rhyme. If it is intended to be serious, go for rhythm, not rhyme.

Shape poems. Shape poems are easy and look very effective. There are number of garden creatures whose shape lends itself to this work e.g. worms, snails, caterpillars. Make a list of words to describe the movement, colour, touch, pattern and sound of these creatures. Now suggest what they look like i.e. image.

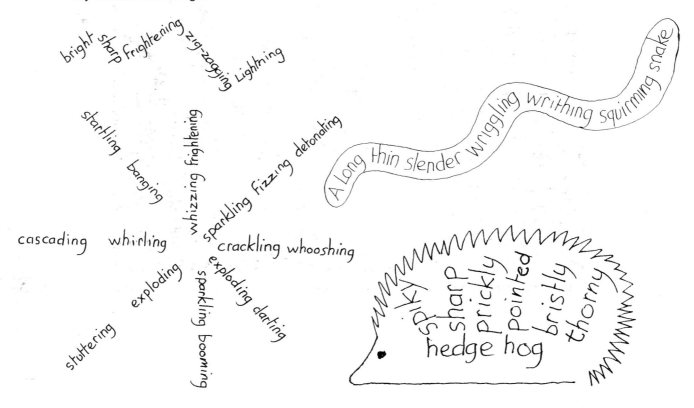

Put your ideas into a snake shape. A poem will grow as you work. Try shape poems for fireworks, hedgehogs, waterfalls, stairs (very useful for not-wanting-to-go-to-bed-poems).

Open the garden gate. Think about the openings which could lead from one world to another: gate, door, drawbridge, portcullis. Make two lists, an ordinary one (things which can be seen from the window) and a magic one e.g. hairy Hobbits, fire-breathing dragons, a one-eyed Cyclops. Begin your poem with the words 'Open the garden gate/Perhaps you'll see . . .' and contrast your everyday ideas with magic ones. Make your poem ready for display by turning it into an opening poem decorated with felt-tip pens.

Castle/portcullis poems related to a history topic – doors opening to another world

MARBLING

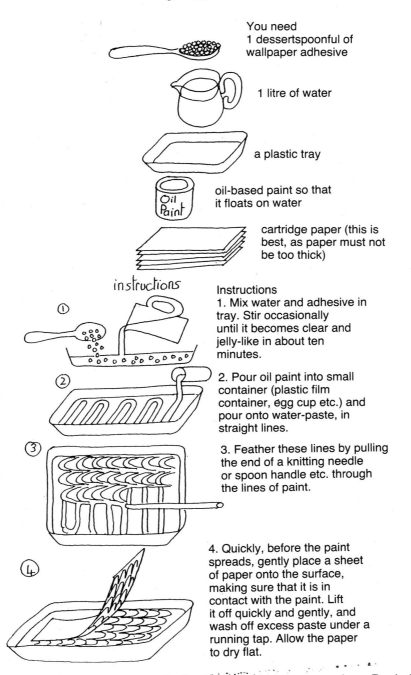

You need
1 dessertspoonful of wallpaper adhesive

1 litre of water

a plastic tray

oil-based paint so that it floats on water

cartridge paper (this is best, as paper must not be too thick)

instructions

Instructions

1. Mix water and adhesive in tray. Stir occasionally until it becomes clear and jelly-like in about ten minutes.

2. Pour oil paint into small container (plastic film container, egg cup etc.) and pour onto water-paste, in straight lines.

3. Feather these lines by pulling the end of a knitting needle or spoon handle etc. through the lines of paint.

4. Quickly, before the paint spreads, gently place a sheet of paper onto the surface, making sure that it is in contact with the paint. Lift it off quickly and gently, and wash off excess paste under a running tap. Allow the paper to dry flat.

The marbling technique can be used effectively for book covers (see Book Cover section on page 52).

For details of further Belair Publications please write to:
BELAIR PUBLICATIONS LTD., P.O. Box 12, TWICKENHAM TW1 2QL, England.